Thoughts,
Prayers,
Reflections

Thoughts, Prayers, Reflections

A collection of talks broadcast on Radio Two and Four and on World Service for the BBC by Peggy Makins (formerly Evelyn Home)

British Broadcasting Corporation

Published by the
British Broadcasting Corporation
35 Marylebone High Street, London W1M 4AA
ISBN 0 563 17634 2
First published 1979
© Peggy Makins 1979

Printed in England by
Whitstable Litho Ltd., Whitstable Kent.

Contents

Foreword — Explaining Myself

Everyone who broadcasts for the BBC's Religious Department must express his own belief, and mine is not orthodox Christianity, or orthodox anything. Indeed for years I felt that the generally acknowledged Almighty God was a thoroughly nasty character, inferior morally to almost any of his creatures – assuming, of course, that he existed.

I did not confuse the Almighty with Christ. It seemed plain that the ineffectual but lovable Jesus I had learned about in Sunday School and church had none of the overbearing cruelty of the real ruler of the world. But neither could one hold him responsible for the pattern of earthly life; his own teaching was always directing one's gaze to the Kingdom of God which was well away from the mess, disease and suffering of ordinary existence, and it was this mess that needed explanation. As least it did – and still does – to me. I needed a God who accepted the responsibility for all things sordid and despicable as well as bright and wonderful; Jesus could not fill that role.

I tried being an atheist, but after a short period of euphoria discovered that the facts didn't fit it. Maybe the universe has come about by accident (though no one could prove it) but why then the general human sense that there is a rightful order of things? It is a sense shared by all societies; tribal morals may differ, but all, however savage-seeming to us, have grown out of the desire to make an orderly, tolerable and continuing life for the greatest number. Why, if we are just accidentals, do we cling so tightly to existence – to the experience of pain, disappointment, frustration and sorrow which makes up such a large part of our days? For the sake of the love, the ecstasy, the pleasure which make up the smaller part? But if love is another accident, how does something so intangible grow out of a material mix-up? How have our awareness, our judgment emanated from solids, liquids and gases?

Human beings in general have a sense of purpose and good which doesn't seem to go with an accidental universe, although, of course, it may do. But I decided to try the experiment of blaming the world on God, the ruling spirit, and the first section of the experiment was to pray.

I prayed because those who believe most strongly in God recommend prayer. I didn't make up a picture of a god to pray to; I sent my thoughts into emptiness and expected no answers.

But answers came; the experiment worked. The painful world began to make sense, though not the sense I'd expected. I didn't become a churchgoing Christian, though increasingly I turn to Christ for example and inspiration.

I have not settled into being a member of anything more dogmatic than the Society of Friends, and of those I am a fairly eccentric Quaker.

This is the background of opinion in which I write and broadcast for John Lang and his team of laymen and priests who make up the BBC's Religious Department. They have helped me a great deal, not only in teaching me the technique of speaking into a microphone and using the sort of words a wide audience will understand, but in the practice of religious awareness. They never forget God.

The other helpers I must thank are the millions – yes, there were that many – the millions of people with problems who wrote to me when I was the magazine *Woman*'s Evelyn Home, and who showed me how love works and part of what it is. Only a part because love is God, and we could not take in the totality of it even if we were shown it.

This first trio of 'Thoughts' was almost my first ever.

I called them 'The Bad Days'.

The Bad Days

Admitting Defeat

The sort of day I need a thought for is one of those hectic, horrible ones either full of anxious, hopeless, waiting, or stuffed with ordeals, major and minor, or so tightly scheduled that I'm bound to let someone important down who'll never forgive me. Your brand of horrible day may be different, but mine turns up so frequently I just have to do something about it.

From a lifetime of answering other people's problems I've learned that the important thing when you're near wits' end is to admit that you need help. The truly un-aidable person is the one who says: 'It's no good asking anyone for advice or listening to what people tell you, there's nothing to be done. All I can do is bear it alone.' That effectively shuts you out from any improvement in the situation.

I proved the point myself once years ago when my mother was dying slowly and painfully of cancer.

Her illness created a lot of extra work and worry. The war had just started, I was newly engaged, holding down a demanding job in London and a demanding job, too, looking after Mother's country pub. My elder brother had gone into the forces, I was trying to make my little brother feel happy and secure, but feared I wasn't succeeding. I had no proper time to attend to office work, I couldn't ease Mother's pain or satisfy her wishes, the pub and its customers created endless problems with new wartime regulations, there were no staff to be had, I had no time for love or sleep or hope.

I remember one morning early, standing on the landing outside my mother's room before going in to greet her and saying fiercely; 'It's too much for me, it goes on and on and on. How am I expected to cope?'

It was not a pious thought; it was defiant, outraged. I hadn't been praying, I'd been complaining, but rude as the manner had been, I'd also uttered a genuine cry for help. I'd admitted defeat. I hadn't realised that in coming to the end of my own resources, and recognising the fact, I had at last allowed a spirit of infinitely greater resource than mine to take over. I didn't expect any answer to my cry, but I got it – like a slosh of cold water over the mind. It was not phrased in words, but there was no mistaking this message.

'What are *you* fussing about' it conveyed brusquely: 'Isn't it your mother who's coping with a real trouble? What's wrong with you?'

My knees shook with the force and clarity, but my wits revived. The priorities slipped into their correct order; I recognised my own self-pity, bewailing the loss of the leisure and pleasure which had come so frequently to me all the years of my young life. Wasn't I old enough, yet, at twenty-three, to shoulder an adult's burdens?

Well, it was one of my first lessons, but it doesn't mean I've learned it. Today I'm just as likely to wake up with the old sense of harassment, the sureness that it'll be a day of failure, that it's all hopeless – then I'll run up the Mayday signal again and wait, keeping quiet, to know what I must do. This waiting time is essential; if I start trying to answer my own SOS, heaven leaves me to it.

So if the outlook today seems thoroughly rotten, give up vainly worrying and ask for help, not specifying any particular miracle but living alertly, ready for the coming aid. Often this is all we'll need, the certainty that something good is on the way. It will bring us safely to bedtime and the bad day will be over.

Minute by Minute

My thoughts this week are for the bad days – the days when you wake up unwilling to face the next twenty-four hours, when to look forward seems nothing but torment. I said yesterday that my method on these all-too-frequent occasions is to ask help – whether from God, the higher self, my guardian angel, or what, I don't know. I haven't found that it matters much.

What matters is to admit that I'm inadequate to the situation and must have aid. And I wait for some heavensent suggestion about how to cope. Sometimes all that happens is that in waiting for the suggestion, the day flows past carrying me with it – but sometimes I get instructions.

Recently, for instance, I've had back trouble which made sitting down no longer a nice rest, but a thoroughly nasty pain. One morning, when every movement was a mistake, I faced a day of railway travel; and I'd already discovered train seats must have been specially designed as instruments of torture to my vertebrae. The prospect reduced my cowardly spirit to a whimper. 'I'll never stick it,' I said to myself, 'but I've absolutely promised to go. How on earth will I get through?' I know, it's trivial compared to the massive torments of others, but anyone who's had sciatica will understand. So also my guardian angel.

'Just take it minute by minute,' came the message, firm, calm, sensible. This order, if thought out, means brush your teeth; put on your clothes, check that you've got your ticket, give full attention to every detail, no wandering imagination.

Oh, and I'd brought some pain killers, they'd help on the return journey. I kept them as a treat to look forward too.

On the first train, I unexpectedly met a friend; talking to her helped me ignore the backache, and it was good to know it could be ignored. I felt more optimistic on the next express, where there was a refreshment buffet and my thriller turned out to be excellent. Also I could stand in the corridor from time to time and practise my waistline exercises.

Taking it minute by minute the day passed. It was full of pain, there was no miracle, but then I didn't need one. That night I thanked heaven it was over; no one had been let down, and what I'd done once, I could do again. I admit there's no thrill to the incident; all I am saying is that when you can see no way to proceed, ask and the way becomes clear. I've never been expected to be heroic, just obedient. If I choose to ignore the message, I can. I did just that not so long ago.

I'd been rather ill one night, a bit dramatically. I thought, actually, I'd been poisoned, and when I felt much better next morning, I felt I ought to go to the office where there was an important job to do. I wasn't sure I knew what was commonsense in this case; I asked for guidance and got it – 'Stay at home, you clot', it said. I shrugged it off, and went to London.

There I was ill again, had to have a car home, upset a lot of people's arrangements, created havoc all round and felt a fool.

Now maybe one's higher common sense or super-ego does all this, and it's nothing divine at all. That's quite irrelevant just now – all I'm saying is that this method of coping with near-desperation works; I'm not trying to prove divinity. And if you try it too, and are told 'Take it minute by minute', argue at your peril. Minute by minute is the way life happens; for once you'll go with it knowingly, trustingly, and be brought to peaceful haven in the end.

Ask for Aid

I hope you've wakened up well this morning, full of welcome for the hours to come. But what if you haven't? What if it's a hopeless prospect, nothing but worry, unpleasantness, pain, boredom or worse lying in wait? Is there anything to be done or must you simply grin and bear it? I think there *is* something and I know it *can* work.

I'm suggesting, as I've suggested before, that you acknowledge straight away your own helplessness, and ask for aid to make you able to face whatever's in store. Not to worry about whether you believe in God or Jesus or any other deity; that's not the point. The point is that you can't manage on your own; accept it, and ask the emptiness for aid.

Then listen. Don't try to answer your own SOS, give up the rueful conviction that only a return to the age of miracles can ease your lot, be silent and ready to receive. Sometimes this listening, as I've said, will see you through the day; sometimes you may get, as I do, a sense that the way to live is minute by minute – and sometimes another plan is offered.

Make a bundle of all your fears and hand them over; never mind to whom or to what. Offer the pain, the anxiety, the terror and despair as if you were laying them on a table or an altar. You have nothing else to give, so you give your troubles.

Include all of them; that's important. Think them through carefully, it may even be a good idea to write them down. And what happens?

Well, in my case (and I've done this thing very often, and not only for myself, this listing of items in a load), I invariably come upon just one muddle I can straighten by myself, something that I can start on right away.

An apology it might be, which has been niggling away at my pride, but which would clear the air a bit. Or some definite act I've been putting off in a cowardly way because it might involve me in fuss – you know the sort of thing, returning faulty goods to a store, or making a justifiable complaint to a sharp-tempered neighbour – this sort of funk often shows up as a first stumbling block between me and peace of mind. Well, I may not have strength for the whole day, but I'll clear away this one little matter, I think – and I go forth to act.

Once on the job, even if it's not quite plain sailing, I realise that it's also not the ordeal I'd expected; maybe the neighbour is annoyed, but as I'm not, the dialogue gets somewhere. The shop may hate taking the goods back, but it's a reasonable complaint and once I'm in the discussion I forget all my dread of ill-temper and recover a lot of confidence.

What, in fact, seems almost the literal result of spiritually unloading a burden is that duties and tasks don't disappear, but the heaviness goes out of them. There is no drag holding you back from tackling them; once you jettison the notion of a load upon you, what has looked like a packing case full of iron bars turns out to be a cardboard box stuffed with blown-up balloons.

But will this method work with something very serious – like bereavement or bankruptcy or an illness? Yes, I believe it will, but it is not usually in cases like this that people need to admit to themselves they are insufficient and need help. One wry advantage of being a failure, or a casualty or a mourner is that you are *aware* you can't manage alone; your whole being calls out for help. What help you are given may vary; it can just be a nurse who looks in at the right moment, a bird who sings at sunset, but it comes.

After the bad days, it was natural to consider their opposite – the good and splendid ones – and then the Thoughts became more personal.

I have always wondered why, with so many talents, some people never manage to enjoy being themselves, and here are the answers. Plus some musings on the great blanket differences between men and women – not the physical differences, but the different ways in which opppsite sexes see and manage life.

The Good Days

Splendid Surprises

Maybe you haven't had a minute to think about it yet – but perhaps today is going to be one of those splendid surprises life seems to have up its sleeve occasionally – a truly good day.

There's no accounting for them is there?

You wake up, everything's just the same as usual, the kettle makes its ordinary boiling noise, but somehow today it genuinely sings and the water comes piping out of the spout as if it were delighted to be making you a cup of tea. It may be raining when you look out of the window but instead of saying to yourself, 'Wet *again*', you think 'This'll be good for the crops' and not resent it a bit.

Breakfast, train-catching, getting children off to school or settling to your usual chores will seem absolutely right and proper. On days like these all the friction seems to have gone out of life, and you love what you're given easily, and don't wish you were anyone else or had anything more in the world than you have now.

How we all wish they came more often, but I guess they couldn't because what seems to hallmark them is a total lack of *wishing*. 'Yes, but when you stop wishing you stop breathing,' said a doctor to me rather grimly once. 'Show me someone with no wants and he'll be dead.'

Well, perhaps there's truth in that, but I believe we could throw out a whole lot of wishing and still not endanger our lives all that much. All those envious hours I spend peering into shop windows at clothes I can't afford on models whose slenderness makes me grit my teeth. All those green-eyed admiration sessions in neighbours' new kitchens fitted with the latest gadgets – in spite of the fact that they'd fuse all the wiring in my ancient galley. I basically know I'm better off in comfy jerseys and slacks and coaxing good food out of a basic stove, but usually I can't help wanting something better.

When wanting leaves me alone for a day all of a sudden everything I have is valuable; the old pots and pans give me the pleasure they gave when I had them as wedding presents, people in the street look like friends, I expect nothing but good and good everything is.

Of course I know health has a lot to do with these wonderful occasions; for once there's no pain in the back or spot on the nose or upset liver to make one conscious of every minute that passes. Also I'm sure that old blessing, a clear conscience, is an enormous help, and I'm not talking about being spotlessly pure or anything exaggerated like that. Just that having no quarrel with anyone, no grudges or guilty twinges is so comfortable; when you've forgiven yourself and everyone else seems to have forgiven you, you can enjoy the present moment as if it were just that – a present. As I say, it can happen any time – even today. It can indeed.

Just an Ordinary Day

During the war when a lot of us were always lonely and often miserably anxious, a general complaint was that every day was exactly the same as every other, unless of course it was worse. And it seems to me that this idea of days being uniformly grey still exists and can take all the joy out of life if we let it. Yet is it valid? Can life become just a drab slab of concrete, the same whether you turn it any side up?

Well have you ever looked carefully at a river on a dull day? At first you'd say it was all grey like the sky, well grey-green perhaps. Then grey-green with a few brownish shadows where it passes under trees, then, of course, you'd have to add just a fleck of yellow, almost gold really, where a leaf is reflected in the water, and there is a distinct hint of silver-blue in the eddy by the bridge. And before you know where you are, you're having to mix up all the colours in the rainbow to paint that uniformly grey river.

And I believe that uniformly dull grey days are like it, a

mixture of many colours, with almost always a glint of gold or a hint of Madonna blue to brighten them up – if you watch for it.

Well during one wartime stint which seemed particularly monotonous I began deliberately searching for the bright colours in each day of the week, and I found them.

Starting on Monday, that devil of a day, I always went to a keep fit evening class which pepped me up and put spring into my step. Tuesdays I always got a new book or two from the library, Wednesdays I lunched with a friend who always made me laugh, Thursdays were the days usually when post arrived from my husband and brother overseas, and Fridays – well, Fridays were pay day, glory be. Saturdays were blissfully at home, no trains to catch, everyone knows how good Saturdays can be, and Sundays were peace, with walks by the river or in the woods and the meat ration to roast, and Monday, yes Monday to look forward to.

Oh well, you can always do that artificial cheerfulness stuff I can imagine people saying. But the real point is that it's the *gloom* which is artificial, not the cheer.

The fabric of most ordinary days is full of interest or companionship, comfort or concentration on a job, or a pastime. You enjoy your meals, you see the sun out of the window, or you can put up an umbrella against the rain.

I believe we're too ready to discount regular things as monotonous and trying; perhaps to suggest that we should be thankful for just ordinary days is too much on an ordinary day. But it doesn't do any harm to bear it in mind when that old grey gloom nonsense raises its ugly head.

Red Letter Days

I'm talking about the good days in life, because I don't know whether it's occurred to you too, but they can seem to present more difficulties than you might imagine.

Take the proverbial red letter days, the ones people call the happiest in your life – you know, your wedding or your coming of age, Christmas Day with presents when you're a child, your birthday or the day your beloved's coming home safe after a long parting. How you look forward to these wondrous occasions, building up expectation upon expectation, letting your mind dwell in ecstasy on how gorgeous it's all going to be till the present moment hardly exists and nothing seems to matter but the future.

And then the day itself comes, and so often, although nothing goes wrong with it, it just isn't the miracle it was going to be. Instead of reaching the summit of the mountain at sunrise, you're still among the foothills, the feast upsets your tummy, your lover is just a person, though you still love him, a person like any other person.

It's a mistake, I suppose, ever to lose sight of the fact that the only way to live life to the full is minute by minute, never too much in anticipation. All that expectancy is so full of selfishness really; how lovely I'll look in my white satin and pearls, what super things people are going to give *me*; even *my* sweetheart is coming home and bother you, Jill. *I* am going to be stuffed with good things – result, I get emotional indigestion.

It's unfortunate that just as self-pity is a terribly painful feeling, it makes any suffering twice as hard to bear, so is self-congratulation. You may deserve every jot of enjoyment in store for you, but if you wallow about in the thought of it beforehand, you'll spoil the actual treat. Like the cook who eats so many glacé cherries and raisins as she's making the Christmas pudding that when it comes to table, flaming with its brandy, she'll have no appetite for it.

On the other hand, of course, it's almost impossible when there is some splendid event in store, to avoid dreaming about it. So what do you do to avoid taking all the gilt off the gingerbread before you've had one bite?

I found myself thinking about this a lot at one time because I used to suffer from migraine, and getting all worked up in anticipation of some gorgeous treat absolutely infallibly brought on one of those filthy headaches which wrecked the whole thing.

On one such day, praying as usual, I found a prayer shaping itself in my head. 'Lord,' I was saying, 'I have too much good in store for me, it's too much for one. Could it please be shared with some others in some way, people who deserve it more than I do?' And shortly after I remembered I ought to ring up a good friend I'd promised to keep in touch with, and had forgotten utterly – thinking about her, talking with her brought everything properly into focus again, made me realise how little my red letter day really mattered. And as a result, it really was red letter.

Holy Days

I've talked about the days that are popularly supposed to be the happiest of your life but today I want to try to climb beyond happiness to the holy days, not those which we now call holidays, but the strange odd occasions when heaven reaches out to earth and we are caught up in the encounter.

Not everyone, I realise, has the luck to experience such things; the only reason I can imagine for my being one of them is that for years I battered away in my prayers asking why an all-powerful, all-knowing, all-good God should have needed to create a greedy, pain-ridden world. Then one day I came upon a book by an American called John Macmillan, a healer – a reluctant healer, he called himself. He sounded deeply religious and at the time I was being plagued by hay fever, and I mean plagued.

I'd no idea whether he was genuine, but I wrote for an appointment and was still mildly unconvinced whether or not to be treated by him as I walked away from his consulting rooms. It was a windy day, leaves blowing down the London street; I found myself thinking, 'I could pray about this, after all God's supposed to love me.' It was a sceptic thought, but as it came I was aware of being lifted up on a tide of love, warm, tingling, buoyant. Love was all round me, even within me, I breathed it, felt it animate me.

Instantly I loved everything, everybody, evil and dirt vanished, I saw them transfigured into necessities; in the vital stream of love moved the whole universe.

For three weeks after that holy day I felt I walked with my feet inches above the ground, my mind working furiously on the new notion of evil as the reverse of the coin of good, one inseparable from the other. It is a fruitful subject for thought, this; what, I started asking, is the real nature of evil?

And now to my second holy day. As before it came through my healer friend – who, by the way, never cured my allergies but rather made me see them as the mere nuisance they were.

I was puzzling still on pain and suffering; on the meaning of life, satisfied as I was and am still that love is its mainspring.

One morning I was coming up the long escalator at a London underground station. At the bottom of it I was in a mental fog, somewhere in the centre the fog lifted, and with perfect clarity I saw that nothing was unplanned, nothing at the mercy of evil, no one forgotten and nothing was finished. It was all beginning, death itself especially.

Later reading Alan Watts's *The Way of Zen*, I recognised the experience as enlightenment; not an answering of questions, but a realisation that there is an answer, to be gradually unfolded perhaps, or just to be joyfully accepted.

From time to time since then I have had glimpses of both experiences again, and in them I live.

Enjoying Yourself

Self-Knowledge

I was once asked very suddenly, at the end of a meeting, what I thought was my main purpose in life. Choking back the answer, 'To get away from here in time to catch the eleven fifteen', which was the main purpose of the moment, I heard myself saying, 'To enjoy as much of it as possible, I suppose'. And I think most of us share this ambition whether our tastes run to the high and rarefied, such as ancient Chinese manuscripts or low and earthy such as fish and chips with vinegar.

Yet how do we set about getting our enjoyment?

Not very efficiently, judging from the crying need for more and more social workers, Samaritans, psychiatrists and marriage guidance counsellors, not to mention the thousands of unhappy problem letters which fall on the agony aunties' desks each day.

People like life all right in theory, but they don't know how to manage it. I certainly don't: I'm always plotting to get myself some treat which then turns to ashes in my mouth, and everyone knows the stories of people like the late Howard Hughes, multi-millionaire, who could have had the whole world, but eventually lost the power of enjoying anything except one old film.

So what cuts us off from satisfaction? How is it that when we can see all the materials of joy around – sunshine, laughter, activity, interest, love, companionship – we are separated from revelling in them by a sort of wall of glass which won't let us get through?

Well, I think the glass wall is part of ourselves, not something from outside. And I believe it is the symptom of a self-hatred which, when it's uppermost, turns our mind bitterly inward and obliterates every other response to people or circumstances.

There's nothing odd, of course, about self-hatred. Very few

of us completely like ourselves, though I suppose there are some smug rarities who wouldn't change a particle from top to toe. But most have some weakness or ugliness which they regret, because they know it is their own fault, and these regrets can take the shine off the most joyous day.

For instance, if you're one of us who detests her or his body for being fat, you'll never enjoy a good tuck-in because guilt at the weakness which won't resist greedy temptation spoils the taste of the dishes. And if you hate yourself for cowardliness, you'll never enjoy going up a mountain on the safe, gradual side, or walking down the steps instead of diving into the swimming-pool.

If only we could excuse ourselves for being chicken or a bit greedy, a spot of indulgence or timidity wouldn't mean a thing. But if we've got some inward high and mighty self-portrait and we fall short of it, we're going to brood and castigate ourselves as if we really were trash.

Of course it's right to know our faults, also to try to cure them. But constant condemning of one's own personality is just another form of egotism, none the better because it's critical and not complimentary. Also it inhibits improvement. The plant which is regularly dug up to see if it's growing soon stops growing; the character which is always being dissected under a microscope has no chance to grow out of faults and develop new qualities.

Yes, self-knowledge is essential, but once a regular fault is recognised, surely the best plan is to make up your mind to reform, pray to be able to do so – and then stop thinking about yourself. The prayer helps, I strongly believe, because it involves the power of the subconscious on which God works. You don't have to agree with me about that, but try the prayer all the same, even if you address it to your super-ego.

I suggest all this because I've done it myself and found it effective.

Not that I've become flawless, roll on the day. But I find I can accept more calmly that I'm ordinary, vulgar, mediocre, and selfish, not proof against temptation and likely to behave as badly as anyone in the world. This acceptance puts the feet firmly on the ground, and I for one, enjoy the security.

Talents

I'm talking about enjoying life, the ordinary aim of the average human being, and how difficult an art it is for a good many of us. One reason for this, I suggest, is that we don't like being ourselves, won't accept our nature and its limitations, and in repining over this miss many a fine experience. Sometimes joy comes as a shock when we think we have no right to it – for instance to those who mourn.

They don't expect to enjoy life, and at first when the fact of death is fresh and dreadful, it is impossible for any other emotion than grief to occupy their minds. I wouldn't argue with the rightness of such pain, and to yield to it is much more healing than to try to suppress it.

But in such depths there can occur moments of wonder and beauty, tokens that the spirit is still alive, and will awaken again to the sun's warmth and the birds' singing. At this point some people begin to hate themselves for their disloyalty to the dead. 'How can I laugh when he's gone?', or 'I must be a shallow beast to enjoy that TV show' – or 'Fancy looking forward to tea when he won't be coming home to share it'.

It is most painful, this self-loathing, in people who had genuinely believed they were inconsolable, and told all their friends they were. Yet there is nothing wrong about natural resilience; it is simply, as Jane Austen once wrote, that some of us have the gift of being ready to be comforted, minds ready to turn from sorrow and find interest and compensation in all circumstances. Why spoil an incomparable gift by hating it?

Bereavement, when we have loved, is perhaps the saddest of all experiences, but it is also a challenge and a revelation. Without the support of a dear partner or parent, we have a moment in which to see ourselves standing upright alone, or cringing at the prospect of the future, and this can be an invaluable vision.

'I realised when he died that I couldn't live alone, I must look after somebody,' said a sixty-five-year-old widow to me. 'It took time to make up my mind, but eventually I sold up and got a job as a cook in this old people's home. I just make myself useful there in all sorts of ways, as well as doing the cooking, and really I quite enjoy it. I'm not actually happy, I suppose, but it's the next best thing.'

That's another point I want to make. Enjoying life is not the same as being happy, although those who are happy enjoy life. But the happy by nature, I think, have something better than the capacity to be consoled – they always see the ultimate good in the heart of things, even affliction, and no one can ever quench their hope or confidence.

Happiness can't be pursued; it has to be God-given, but enjoying life is largely within our own scope. We can get better at it if we try, and are not put off by our own shortcomings.

A basic step to a proper appreciation of life is a proper appreciation of the equipment we've been given to manage it with. What's that? – well, a body, five senses, if we're lucky, some kind of health, not necessarily good, a mind and spirit, willpower and imagination. With these aids we have to face all the happenings providence sends us – and we need them all.

So it's futile to reject your body, however imperfect, or decry your brains because you're not clever, or write off your willpower because using it takes a lot of effort. Without these qualities you'll have no life to enjoy. Yes, we come back to the talents in the parable. Maybe you haven't been given many, but if they've been practised and developed, the original five may have become ten without your knowing anything except that it's been a good life and you've enjoyed it.

True to Yourself

Enjoying life is an art we can all practise, but it's not as simple as it sounds, because before we can be pleased with anything we have to be pleased to be ourselves, warts and all. And there is within most of us a fastidious portion which won't put up with warts. So we try to forget them, ignore them, leave them out of our picture of ourselves – and get it all wrong.

Take an example. Let's say you, like me, were brought up among people with common vulgar tastes, and your favourite meal is bangers and mash with Worcester sauce followed by golden syrup roll and packet custard. I don't say this is my very favourite meal, but it's good nosh. But since the days when you always had it on Saturdays, you've been climbing the social ladder into a higher class who look down on Worcester sauce and golden syrup roll. At least you think they do, because they don't seem to serve it much at dinner parties.

So to keep up with the nobs, we deny our vulgar tastes, outlaw them, shove them out of sight and reject that part of our nature which still hungers for them. Similarly we wear clothes which conform to high society's fashion notions and instead of watching football or going to bingo, we go racing which bores us stiff, and furnish our house with stuff chosen to impress visitors, not to make us comfortable.

All this double-think takes its toll on our nerves and makes us bad-tempered. What ought to be a thoroughly enjoyable existence becomes a strained, tense, prolonged effort to keep up with an imaginary jet-set image. You can't even enjoy being well-off (which is a lot of people's definition of enjoyment anyway) if you secretly think you're not qualified for the superior life, and you hate your voice, gestures, manners and preferences so much that you're never relaxed in company.

Rich or poor, you must basically accept yourself cheerfully if you're going to find cheer in living.

Not that there's any harm in trying to make improvements. If smoothing out your accent appeals to you, then have a go at it by all means. If you'd like to appreciate good music and pictures, study the arts, go to classes, develop discrimination, but to please yourself – don't hope to impress others or you'll get nothing out of the effort.

Enjoying life means accepting your tastes, refining them if it comes naturally, but getting His Highness to order bangers and mash with Worcester sauce at the Ritz next time he takes you to dinner, if that's what you really fancy.

To like being oneself means being true to oneself, and true to every vulgarity as well as every more noble inclination – but once you begin to enjoy life as yourself, you seem to find more and more things to enjoy. The only music you liked used to be pop, perhaps, but you discover some classics which thrill you, and pieces from opera which bring a lump to your throat, and you read more of the newspapers than the headlines and the horoscopes and your TV watching becomes wider still and wider.

Give yourself a chance and you'll find quiet interest in watching people, in thinking things out, in wondering at what sort of God made both pain and ecstasy and ourselves. And if for a second we can see ourselves as indispensable to God and man, the one piece which fits the gap in the jigsaw, we shall never again suffer that crushing sense of inferiority which generates self-hatred, and hating everyone else as well.

You'll remember, of course, that hackneyed piece about loving your neighbour as yourself; it's a lot easier to accept him or her, with all his peculiarites, if first you've accepted and come to value your own.

Content to be You

I've been talking about enjoying life, which starts with enjoying being yourself – not smugly, for heavens' sake, but acknowledging all handicaps and nastinesses, and still feeling content, even thankful, to be you.

I am put to shame, of course, by those who achieve serenity although they are disabled, in chronic pain, or poor, oppressed or cruelly victimised for their convictions. Even so, I enjoy life more than I used to, and I enjoy being myself more.

One of the things that has helped me is the knowledge, as I grow older, that everyone is more than himself or herself. He or she is also an effect on the universe, never a name writ in water. Take the case of one of those castaways on Roy Plomley's desert island, parted from every other human soul: the moment he tears down a few palm branches to make a shelter, he's having an effect on the fauna of the island. When he massacres some fish to fry for lunch he is altering the balance of ocean life. He may not be able to influence anyone human, but he is an influence all the same.

Take a badly handicapped boy I once met. He had every excuse for hating being himself, but he suffered neither from self-disgust nor self-pity. Physically he was much less than the average person, but in his effect on those around him he was a giant. He brought forth saintliness, generosity, ingenuity, good humour, devotion and gratitude from the most unlikely people. He may have had a hate-worthy body, but in accepting it and appreciating everything possible, he was not only enjoying himself but giving enjoyment to all who contacted him.

They went away, having tried to help or please him, feeling more at peace with themselves, more worthwhile than they had before. The reason, I suppose, that the Mother Teresas of this world can do their work is that in the most unworldly way, they enjoy it, because it gives no excuse for self-hatred. And they love the poor and dying because these people provide them with the inestimable privilege of giving love, which is also the greatest pleasure.

Mind you I don't think we dare credit ourselves with the fine qualities we bring out in others. Otherwise my great-grand-uncle Jim whose drunkenness led to three generations of teetotallers might be considered almost a saint.

Not that Jim lived to see any results of his weakness, which is rather unfair – like the case of the unfortunate man in the New Testament whose blindness, healed by Jesus, was said to have been created to make manifest the power of the Lord.

If he was a sensible man, however he would thereafter have concentrated on the glory of being able to see rather than questioning the past.

Best of all, I think, must be to be able always to take oneself cheerfully for granted, and appreciate whatever is going on at the moment. But when life ceases to be fun, when we begin to ask, 'Why am I having such a rotten time? Is it because I'm a rotter?', then maybe it's time to pull up sharply and take stock.

If the cause of the rotten time sticks out a mile – like drunkenness or drug-taking – then the self-loathing which makes many people effect a drastic change in personality is in fact proper self-love. Alcoholism or drug addiction is the outward face of an inner death wish, a desire to escape from oneself. When the inmost will demands the breaking of the habit, the return to health is a sign that there is still life in the soul, which means to survive. Like a cut-down tree, the cured addict grows from one untainted springing new branch.

Vive la différence

Problems with Priorities

For the next four mornings, I shall be talking about something rarely mentioned today, although its kin-word 'sex' seems to be in every headline. I mean the effects of gender; the ways in which men and women differ in looking at the world, God and each other, and how it might help if those views were more often reconciled or respected.

I'd like to start with a very simple example; one of the most frequent irritations of married life for women is the habit of so many men to come home from work, absent-mindedly accept a greeting, then having eaten a meal almost in silence, to sit down in front of the television and go to sleep.

Wives who have spoken to no one of their own age all day except perhaps to say 'Three pints please', to the milkman, feel outraged at this example of neglect. 'I'd love to hear about his work, or talk over the news; *he's* making me a cabbage', one wife said. But she hadn't realised that her husband's job, which meant talking all day, appearing alert, cheerful and efficient was exceptionally tiring to a man who by nature was not very talkative ever. Her Jim had generally used up all his available energy once he got home; he had no intention of neglecting her, hadn't even realised how much he slept. And when she suggested a night or two off to play tennis with her friends and have a natter, he was bewildered. He hadn't seen her view any more than she'd seen his.

Now I've no idea why God or evolution chose to make the continuance of the human race depend on at least a modicum of goodwill and understanding between the sexes, but this is the way things are arranged, and it seems to me that our best chance of happiness is to accept it. Not in the hapless sense of making the best of a bad job, but of enjoying welding the mothering, soothing, peacemaking qualities of women to the

20

audacious, competitive spirit of men. Of course I am generalising; not every man is audacious or competitive, not every woman is motherly, but on the whole, gender makes most soldiers men and most nurses women. The most complete welding is obviously when men and women fall in love, and for a short time see each other as a miracle – and in that state of wonder get married – but don't necessarily live happily ever after.

The trouble is that boys and girls not only have to love and live together in the world, they also have to keep it stocked with their own kind, and this enterprise is work, with only the vaguest tinge of romance.

Family-raising is more, even, than a career; it is like having to eat or drink to remain alive, and practically all women see it that way, but not all men.

Men, it seems, give their hearts first to some kind of activity which will become their lifework, they hope. 'I want to drive racing cars', or 'I want to have a farm', or perhaps 'I don't know what I want to do' – but never, 'I want to be a husband and father'. Whereas girls begin with loving children, often their own little brothers and sisters, and a majority will say, 'Well, eventually I want to be a wife and mother.'

Talented people are lucky in that both men and women realise that musicians, actors, artists are liable to put their professions first in life. But ordinary couples have more difficulty in seeing each other's point of view. It is hard for a wife to understand why the apparently dull office her husband goes to, and possibly grumbles about, every day is still to him as vital as the children she tends and tries to make into good citizens. And he is much more likely to see them as simply ordinary kids than ever she is, and wonder why she fusses so much about them.

When a couple can respect each other's priorities without quarrelling or questioning, they will both have a little more sympathy for everyone in God's world who is so different from everyone else.

Emotional Props

I'm talking this week about the different view of life as seen by ordinary men and women, and one of the most noticeable differences concerns smoking and drinking. Whenever statistics are given about alcoholism or chain smokers, the vast majority of victims are men, although it is usually reported that the number of women at risk is increasing.

Men have always liked some kind of rose-coloured glass through which to see hard facts – a glass of something intoxicating for preference – which means that although there are plenty of abstemious men, and women who over-smoke and over-drink, the pubs are still largely inhabited by men who enjoy their leisure better for being a bit lit up, tobacco and liquor-wise.

One of the most divisive factors in marriage is this different value set by husbands and wives on the soothing drugs. I remember a man saying in my pub on a budget day years ago, 'Another penny on beer and smokes – they're my only pleasure and the wife grudges me 'em as much as the dratted Chancellor' – and I wondered what on earth could be so delightful about a mouthful of smoke mixed with the sourish taste of beer.

Now I know that what these two luxuries give is what men seem to long for regularly more than anything else – extra confidence. I don't believe most of them long to escape the harsh reality of their surroundings as much as they want to escape the harsh reality of themselves. With the help of being mildly drunk which makes a little wit go a long way, with the illusion of sophistication given by tobacco smoke, a man can ignore the brute fact that he is just average, not very good at anything, not likely ever to be a great success. With the alcohol and nicotine comforters he can at least see himself as a bit of a devil – a far more satisfactory image.

Women, the practical, unromantic sex (yes, we truly are; one of the saddest discoveries men make is how drearily down-to-earth we are), see booze and smoking as extravagances, frivols – not as morale-boosters.

And men, for their part, rarely appreciate what beauty aids do for women. The hairset which makes a plain girl feel pretty, the slimming food that costs twice as much as ordinary grub, but which convinces Mum she is going to be a sylph again; the creams, lotions, treatments and beauty farms which most men scorn – these, plus clothes, are the alcohol and nicotine of the average female.

A man will give himself a stiff drink before going to an important appointment; a girl traditionally buys herself a new hat, or a whole new outfit.

Deep in all our hearts is a fearful question of our own destiny; what is to become of us, what will be demanded by the God who we hope loves and cares for us, but who moves in ways beyond our understanding? When we are forced to face this question most of us need some kind of prop, something to lean on while we are forced to assess our human condition and reckon how little, on the whole, we are worth.

Men at this moment take a shot of forgetfulness and Dutch courage; women attempt to transform their mundane selves into something more beautiful and appealing. When we recognise the reason for each other's silly weaknesses, we find it much easier to forgive them – and sometimes, if we are lucky, we feel God forgives us too.

Supernatural Certainties

Talking of the different view of life seen by men and women, I think one might say that intellectuals, brainy people, of both sexes have no use for superstition (although there have always been stories about great financiers who consult crystalgazers before committing big deals).

Leaving out this élite, most ordinary men and women believe strongly in luck – but whereas men, on the whole, feel that good luck may be just around the corner, women tend to be pessimists who know that disaster is always threatening but hope it won't come today. It must be this difference in the attitude towards luck which makes men so much more likely to be gamblers than women.

I remember writing a rather fierce piece against gambling when I was dealing with personal problems as Evelyn Home.

I'd received several miserable letters from women unable to keep the family housed and fed because of the gambling habits of their men, and I felt strongly that this business of trying to get something for nothing and almost invariably getting less than nothing as a result was just plain daft.

Plenty of people wrote agreeing with my piece, but one man's letter was a gentle reproof. 'I'm not a great gambler,' he wrote, 'I assure you the biggest sum I ever put on the pools is fifty pence. But that buys my licence to dream. Without it, I'd have no right at all to think about a new car or giving my wife all the things she wants – so isn't the instinct to gamble a bit religious really? Like believing in miracles or a God who does answer prayers?'

It was a viewpoint I'd not seen: over-romantic, but no more nonsensical than a girl's hope, as she reads her horoscope, that today won't be too bad.

The trouble with male optimism is that it can make a man very dissatisfied with average, reasonable luck (which in the long run works out better for health than a traumatic win on the pools). The top prizes become the only ones worth having, and the urge to keep throwing good money after bad never lets up, even after some minor win.

Yet this persistent hopefulness is, I think, preferable to the frame of mind of the many women who read their stars, consult fortune tellers or get frightened to death by a cross word from a gypsy. Superstition takes from them all use of their own willpower; the stars foretell, and what they have foretold will come to pass. No use trying to gainsay it, all we can do is sit and talk about what's bound to happen and hope it won't be too painful for us personally.

Now it's not entirely silly to be superstitious, because obviously some people do seem to have all the luck. The Bible says that to those that have shall be given, and to those that have not, even that which they have shall be taken away. What troubles most of us is that we are not quite sure which category we belong to; are we the blessed or the deprived? Does being loved by God mean automatically being rich, famous or distinguished? Or does it mean being meek and poor and inheriting the earth?

In an attempt to answer this unanswerable riddle, women pore over their half-column of astrology while men leaf through pages and pages of sports and business reports – all of us seeking to achieve heaven on earth and avoid the wrath of our Creator.

Ordinary people know that in some way – maybe by luck – earth is linked to heaven, and that those who get no shiver of the supernatural by looking at the way life treats us really are, for all their education, pretty dumb.

Different Worlds

I have been talking this week about the different visions of the world seen by men and women. I've said that we ordinary people, by our belief in luck, show that on the whole we recognise the presence of a supernatural force which works on our destiny. But when it comes to putting into practice some kind of acknowledgement of this force very few of us do it by going to church to worship it. But of this very few, by far the larger proportion is female.

Women are always needing help; they are faced throughout life with the necessity to beg for aid even in tiny emergencies like changing a washer, for instance, when they can't unscrew the tap, or changing a wheel when they find, having successfully removed the damaged one, that they can't lift the spare out of its cranny. In more important matters, they usually need help in childbirth, and while tending babies they need protection too.

So a woman sees nothing humiliating in praying to God just to help her carry on day after day, and she visualises church vaguely as a safeguard against all those enemy forces she can do nothing about.

Ordinary working men, however, usually see themselves as self-sufficient and would be ashamed to beg help even of an Almighty God. They pride themselves on standing on their own feet, changing their own washers, and being muscular enough to cope with any spare wheel. It requires infinitely more imagination for them to see the need of a Father in heaven for everyday life, although He might be useful if He'd only see that the right winning number came up in a sweep-stake.

There is a difference too in the way ordinary women and men see authority. Women on the whole (and I'm not speaking for liberationists) regard it as protection, something to lean on and shelter behind. Men, particularly young men, frequently see it as a challenge, to be questioned and flouted. And God as an authority is not very welcome to men.

In fact many of them feel that He really isn't able to carry on by Himself. Unless they organise the church rebuilding or hold evangelistic rallies, poor old God would be forgotten and helpless.

I once went to a very high-up function whose object was to tell reporters what poor publicity the church had been getting lately when it had been showing great tolerance and friendli-ness towards other churches. Every other person at the con-ference was a man and all seemed to feel that without publicity God's church was threatened.

Nothing can really threaten the God that most ordinary women believe in; they can even find comfort in His silence when they pray. Whereas men, who turn to God usually only when they are in great emotional distress, are just as likely to say, like the psalmist, 'Why have you brought all this mis-fortune upon me?' Often they pity female weakness, but when physical strength begins to fail and they grow older, the struggle for them to come to terms with something greater than themselves is like Jacob's long weary wrestling match with the angel.

Both sexes are bound to see different worlds: men an envi-ronment to be subdued and adapted to their will, women a strong, intractable background like the granite wall up which a plant can grow, twining and twisting to keep its hold on exist-ence.

There may come a time for us all when the two visions merge and make one; and then we may be in heaven, where it is reported there is neither male nor female.

'Thought for the Day' can be a philosophical or meditative programme; but sometimes it makes space for neat religion undiluted with ethics or anecdotes. To me the heart of faith lies in prayer, and there is a lot to be learnt about this practice which can only be acquired with the habit of praying. And a surprising number of people cannot bear to pray; they feel ashamed or shy or downright silly, whether or not they go down on their knees.

I felt I'd like to reassure them that there's nothing stupid about praying and give them, as humbly as possible, since I am a beginner in religion, the few facts I've learned from and about prayer.

Primer on Prayer

Learning to Pray

Ever since I woke up to the fact that I believed in God, I have wondered why we are not all possessed of the same kind of conviction, if not in the same kind of deity. Not for any virtuous reason, but because a god worth believing in can be held responsible; it is easy enough to condemn ourselves for some of the world's ills and woes, but when it comes to the earthquake, the tidal waves, the bacteria and the thunderbolts – then even the most human of humanists has to admit that men neither make them nor control them and that something stronger does.

To believe in a God is to find a scapegoat in a guilty world; even when I thoroughly disliked the deity and my prayers consisted of accusations: for instance, 'What do you mean by making life hell for so many innocent people?' it was a relief to be able to lay the blame somewhere.

And from these abstract petitions eventually came the real thing – the prayers that are answered and are a blessing. So this week I am going to talk about the journey towards religious faith on which the first step for me was learning to pray. I doubt whether any two persons would notice exactly the same features on any journey, but some landmarks stand out.

My first real discovery was that I had to confess that I needed help before I could recognise any answer to prayer and that therefore a lot of my arguments with God didn't qualify at all. I was surprised to realise that I'd regarded myself as totally self-reliant and beyond the aid of anyone – until suddenly a situation came up that made me feel incapable of managing by myself.

Briefly it was during the last weeks of my mother's short life when suddenly I had to assume her responsibilities as well as my own, and thought the burden unfairly heavy. 'How am I expected to cope?' I angrily asked heaven – and was shown at once that it was my mother who was really coping with a crisis, facing the loneliness of death, and that I was merely expected to use my youth and strength to help her – a task well within my powers.

Later I learned that this was a very typical answer to prayer – nothing soothing or sympathetic but a sharp dose of reality which cut one down to size and showed a situation in an entirely new light.

I had thought, all those years ago when Mother was ill, that I really was behaving rather well – dashing round finding a second opinion among specialists to try to cure her, sparing an hour or so each day to straighten the routine details of her business, giving a bit more care and attention to my small brother.

But the brusque reply to my involuntary cry for help had shown me that I'd really thought her illness a nuisance, an interruption of my own very interesting young life, a burden laid upon *me* – I hadn't seen the vastly greater burden laid upon her, as she lay facing the unknown, anxious about her children and often in miserable pain.

You might think that prayer is not much of a blessing if this is the kind of thing it shows you about yourself. If all it did was show up weakness, I'd agree – but it also gives one the strength to put things right. Mother and I parted as the most loving friends; I gave her all the affection I could during our last days together – and I think, at any rate I hope, she noticed the difference.

Awaiting the Response

This week I'm talking about prayer not as something vague and abstract but as a regular exercise – and I believe used this way it releases a force anyone can experience, as long as they are prepared first to assume that there is in life a ruling spirit greater than themselves, wiser and more benevolent. When you can say, truthfully, 'Lord, help me, I need you', then you may recognise the aid given.

But even if your humility is real, there is something else about prayer I have noticed – no result will come from the humblest petition if you try to answer it yourself.

Take, for instance, the prayer in the hearts of many would-be parents: 'Dear Lord, please give us a child.' Quite often this prayer seems to be ignored – because it leaves no space for any vision of life which does not include the longed-for cradle. But if the prayer can be an offering of love – 'We have love to give, show us where it is needed' – then I think the response may come clearly, even if it is not in the form of a baby.

To pray and wait, this is one of the exercises which yields results in my experience – though, as I've said, it's hard on the patience, until one realises that the patience is part of the answer.

In fact two of the vain habits which prayer gradually and inexorably weeds out are getting over-tense and constantly worrying.

I was once very het-up indeed about a book I was writing. Far too long had been spent in planning it, then pulling the plan to pieces, for too little actually bashing away at the type-writer. Now I was at a deadline with both the publisher and the wolf at the door at once.

'Oh, Lord,' I said without any reverence whatsoever, 'how am I ever going to get this done?' I didn't expect any answer, but I got one. 'Work harder and stop moaning', it said, to my annoyance. It was right, though; cutting out my regular cries of distress yielded more days than I believed possible, and though I failed the deadline, I beat the wolf in the end.

A similar discovery can be made, through prayer, about worrying.

Take a well-known situation; someone you love is ill, has been taken out of your reach to hospital – the case may be serious. There is nothing you can do, so you worry, you feel you must. Not to do so would seem heartless. Eventually the perpetual strain of waiting for news begins to make you feel ill yourself.

Instead of reacting in this way to the circumstances, try prayer, not for yourself but for the sufferer. 'Dear Lord,' I'd say, 'if my love for Aunt Liza can do anything to help her, I offer it to you on her behalf.' And every time anxiety started I'd repeat the prayer – then peace of mind would take the place of gnawing worry and I might even sit down to write to Auntie so that though out of my reach, she would know eventually I'd been thinking about her.

Suppose the prayer apparently fails; the loved one dies. Isn't it possible that higher authority has said, 'It will be a lot better for Aunt Liza to be with me than battling with the world?' We're always so ready to assume that life is much better than death – our bodies always think this – that it takes prayer to show a new vision. Death may be no punishment, but a treat beyond all treats; in prayer one may glimpse heaven.

Cry from the Heart

Talking about prayer in practice, I've said it doesn't answer very well when we are asking something for ourselves – such as, 'Please Lord, let me pass this examination', or when breathless we pant, 'Please Lord, let me catch the last bus.' The reply to the first petition might well be 'Don't waste time praying, do some more revision,' and to the second, 'Run with all your might.' God is not, on the whole, a magician: his rabbits come out of burrows, not top hats, and the way to stop your foot hurting is not to repeat a hundred paternosters, but to stop and take the stone out of your shoe.

There is, though, a kind of prayer which comes to mind when there is some ordeal to be faced and one has gained a firm trust in a ruling spirit wiser and stronger than oneself.

A friend once told me that to his terror he was going to have to talk to an expert audience about his own faith, and then lead them into a meditation on higher things. He had no notion of how to manage the situation; he never spoke in public, had no confidence in his personality in such a test and above all feared he might destroy the reverence and trust of others if he made a mess of the occasion.

When it came to the point, as the audience gathered, he prayed and was given an inspiration. 'Lord,' he said, 'all I can offer you is my fear and uneasiness, my fright and ignorance.

But if these things can be used for your purpose, please let them be.'

It was the right prayer. He forgot himself completely, spoke to a hundred people as if they were one, and found himself led into spiritual thought which he could communicate as easily as he could breathe.

To offer oneself in a package, as it were, when circumstances are beyond one's ordinary power is a fine illustration of how prayer works.

But it's an idea which doesn't always come to mind; there is no rule which I've discovered that you can substitute for the prayer itself. Trying to turn prayer into a routine, a formula to be followed with your eyes shut, has never worked for me. If I am in a jam, and I shout for help, I won't be able to foretell what kind of help I may be offered.

It may be something very simple about taking life minute by minute, which is, after all, the way everyone has to take life – except that we forget the fact. 'How I'm going to put up with Grandfather in the house for another fifteen years,' somebody said to me recently, 'I don't know. He's so irritating, and so bossy . . . ' But of course no one puts up with anything really for fifteen years, you only live an instant at a time, every experience changes from second to second – a crisis situation taken in seconds becomes endurable. Thinking of it as lasting years creates a doom-laden feeling much worse than the actual happening.

Prayer is a reminder of reality, and once tasted, reality becomes acceptable, even when it is bitter, and preferable to the sweetest illusion. When you know, for instance, that you are careless and forgetful – as I am – at least you begin to read recipes twice over before you sprinkle the flour into the mixing bowl and then discover it should have been oatmeal. Or you bow your head humbly before the anger of someone you've unwittingly let down, because you forgot to make a note of the date of meeting them.

You don't bluster and try to bluff your way through life any more; that's a waste of time anyway, and deceives no one but yourself. You find you can gain from criticism, even when it's given in the nastiest possible tone of voice. It can't possibly be any more stringent than some of the things you've been taught in prayer.

So I am trying to say that when prayer has become a regular exercise there is no real substitute for it. Formal devotion can be as meaningful, I'm sure, as the most spontaneous heartcry, but it will not take the place of the heartcry.

Both Sides of the Coin

At the beginning of these talks about the practice of prayer, I said I wished everyone could share my conviction that there is a God. I realise this sounds smug; it isn't intended to be – I say it only because in nearly forty years of counselling so many people have said or written to me 'You are so lucky to have a faith.'

The faith I have has been fostered by prayer, and to those who are quite certain that there is no use in prayer and no point in religion, I'd reply that if prayer and belief were useless, everyone would have forgotten about them long ago, if indeed they'd ever been discovered. But they never have been forgotten; the appetite for God is as great today as it has ever been, and once felt it cannot be ignored.

I am well aware I have not described or named the ruling spirit I pray to, even in the lovable form of Jesus of Nazareth. I stand in awe of the Almighty and like the Jews of old, admit that He is an incomprehensible mystery – but if I can't know Him, he certainly knows me.

To those who say: 'But you can't pray to a God you don't know' (and enclose a pamphlet about their own) I can only repeat that to acknowledge a higher authority than oneself is quite enough as a start, and one learns as one prays.

But if one never becomes on familiar terms with Omnipotence, one is taught some of the effects of His power.

If ever I have prayed for help in some crisis connected with another person, it has come in the form of a rush of vital energy, renewed when asked for, but fading as soon as the need ceases. A member of Alcoholics Anonymous would, I think, receive the same kind of aid in seeing a fellow-member through the prolonged torment of doing without drink – a kind of glowing patience, making steadfastness possible long after ordinary resolution would have failed.

If, on the other hand, I've asked for aid in overcoming some weakness of my own, I've merely had a grim reminder that having recognised the pitfall I needn't throw myself into it. I've probably had more tickings-off from the practice of prayer than from my best enemies, yet I go back gladly for more and only wish I could be more regularly aware of the Holy Spirit and its plans and purposes.

However, even when I'm stolidly conscious of nothing but humdrum routine, I've come to believe that the soul is bound to be in contact with its ruler – it's comforting, this thought, like a child going peacefully to sleep in a darkened room knowing Mother is sitting by the fire downstairs. But to be awake to the spirit and sensible of its love is such bliss that only saints have known how to express it.

There are many inexpressibles in religion; so of course I try to express them. The times, for instance, when one feels new-born, very small, but unshadowed, bright with hope and unworried about anything – death, pain, sin or suffering. At such times one seems to see both sides of the coin at once; the evil that is just the reverse of good, the sorrow which is simply the negative of joy, the opposites that divinity welds into a whole.

And there is just one final bit of knowledge I've gained; before many prayers one has to ask to mean what one says. It was St Augustine, they say, who prayed: 'Make me good, but not just yet.' When tempted to ask to be perfect, it's as well to say first: 'Lord, make me sincere when I ask for this.' You never know, prayers are granted every day.

Here are a couple of 'Thoughts for the Day', intended strictly for Evelyn Home, the agony auntie side of my life.

I answered them exactly as I would have answered letters, except of course that to have problems so succinctly described was a very great improvement on most of the agony letters, which wandered in all directions before coming to the point!

Problems for Evelyn Home

An Unmarried Woman

Announcer: It's a quarter to eight. 'Thought for the Day' this morning comes from a lady in London who writes:

'I am thirty-two next week and the thought occurs that I may never marry. Many people seem to think that unmarried women are failures. I don't feel a failure in any other way, but my friends, I can see, feel sorry for me. Do I have to marry just to prove I'm as good as the next girl?'

Here's Evelyn Home:

This is a question from an unusual girl – a usual girl, I'm certain, would not at the age of thirty-two just start thinking that she might not marry. A usual girl would have been panic-stricken at age seventeen, and if she stayed single, would have known by thirty-two that only a very worthwhile man indeed was going to attract her – or, alternatively, that she really didn't much want a man in her life at all. Or, of course, she might have come to the conclusion that she didn't want a *husband* – just a man might be a rather different proposition.

So we are dealing with an untypical girl. And you'll notice that her real problem is not being unmarried.

She has been single now for almost half her Biblical lifetime (do you realise that the Bible firmly makes you middle-aged at thirty-five?) and it hasn't bothered her at all. Presumably she's had a satisfying job or a very good life at home with her family, and what is upsetting her now is not any change in those circumstances at all, but the fact that her friends seem to be sorry for her.

Her problem is to make her friends stop pitying her, and how well I know the irritation of this. I myself didn't marry until I was twenty-three, which of course isn't thirty-two, but it was still, even over thirty years ago, considered running it rather close to the danger-line, if you wanted to get married.

35

And I well remember the aunts and neighbours saying, 'Twenty-two? Engaged? No? Goodness, you'll have to hurry up won't you if you mean to get married.'

I used to say coldly, 'I don't mean to get married', and I meant it. I didn't like what most of them meant by marriage – a homebound, entirely maternal, domestic life, and I had no intention of living it. When I said so, they didn't believe me – when I married, they were sure I'd reform, but what with a very understanding and delightful husband and fate taking a hand I never have lived a particularly domestic or maternal life and I've enjoyed every minute of it, though in some ways it has been much more like a single woman's life than a wife's.

So why should a single girl, happily occupied for over thirty years of her life, suddenly start taking notice of what friends say? They must have been saying it for at least ten years anyway. Either she herself has recently noticed an attractive male who didn't return her notice, or a friend's children have made her ask herself, 'Wouldn't I like babies of my own?' or someone has been truly bitchy and made her feel sorry for herself for the very first time.

If she has just come alive to the charm of men, they will soon come alive to hers; a girl who *really* never notices men does get overlooked. But a responsive girl, a girl who smiles at men's jokes, perks up at their chatter and shows she likes them will soon have men friends of her own and partnership can follow, whatever her age.

If she is suddenly yearning for babies, I'd beg her to analyse her feelings very honestly and if necessary consider changing her job to one where she may meet more children or work among them. Plenty of women adore children but are a lot cooler about men; to marry a man just to be given children isn't really fair, I'd say – unless, of course, he is marrying for precisely the same reason.

Finally, if some malicious remark has just penetrated an otherwise unbroken contentment, I'd say 'Why take notice of bitchiness?' Some unhappy people – men as well as women – hate the sight of someone living a satisfactory life. Real friends would be pleased at the sight of such satisfaction, though they might be uneasy if it verged on smugness.

The point really is for a thirty-two-year-old bachelor girl to know what she herself wants in life, and what sort of person she really is. If she recognises herself as fortunate, if she honestly feels no lack in her existence – why take any notice of what others say? No one should marry to prove anything to anybody – the reason for marrying is the wish to make someone else happy and to be good to them for life.

Honour and Obey

Announcer: 'Thought for the Day' comes from a listener in the Midlands who writes: 'Although my husband insisted that I promise to "obey" in our wedding service, in fact he refuses to accept responsibility or make family decisions. What can I do, if anything, to encourage him to take the lead sometimes?'

Here with her view about that question is Evelyn Home.

I'm glad about that 'if anything'; it means that the wife who asked the question realises she's got a very hard row to hoe; I hope it means too that she grins to herself when she thinks back to that time when her fiancé insisted she should obey. Probably that was the decision of his life; having summoned up the energy to make it he sank gratefully back into indifference where he hopes to rest for ever more.

But is he, in fact, so supine? Did his wife choose his job for him? Or take over all the responsibility of choosing and paying for their home? Or buy the car and see about its tax and insurance? Or was she so overwhelmed – as most of us women are – with more immediate domestic decisions that she didn't even notice that these large ones were being taken automatically by her irresponsible husband?

Obviously I don't know the answer in the case quoted; I do know, though, that in the thousands I've come across in my *Woman* mail, what has usually exhausted a wife's patience is the need to make literally dozens of small decisions every day without the slightest aid – indeed often with considerable hindrance – from husband and children. And then on top of these things – what to have for dinner, whether to spend the money on Tom's shoes or Greta's socks – on top of all this, to have to make up the family's mind about where to go for a holiday, whether to paint the outside of the house, what to do about Tom's laziness at school. It's all too much. 'If only', the woman thinks, 'he'd just settle for once about the holidays. But if I left it to him we'd never go anywhere.'

I might have said this sort of thing myself, but because I've always worked outside the home, like the average husband, I've known why many a man would never lift a finger to arrange a family holiday. It is simply that for him to be able to stay at home, where he is truly comfortable, to have the sort of meals he likes, to amble down to the pub when he feels like it, or perhaps have a round of golf, would be a holiday of the best kind. Why should he bother making a decision about something he doesn't much want anyway? It's his wife who wants it – let her cope with it.

It's surprising how many of the choices to be made are about home affairs; matters which fall fairly naturally into a wife's half of the shared life of marriage. They're part of her job; it may never have occurred to her that in *his* job, her husband may make just as many small, but necessary decisions as she does about the house. When he comes home, he's tired to death of making up his mind (I once read that it takes as much energy to make a decision as it does to jump a five-foot ditch). There is this also; a man's job may involve no decisions at all, just repetition, drugging, monotonous, soul-destroying. He may be so fatigued and dulled by it that his mind is simply not capable of selection, especially after overtime. A wife's job may be very very hard, but it is not monotonous and soul-destroying, at least while she has young children with her.

So what does this wife do to make her husband take the lead? I'd say – nothing very much, unless she's really very unhappy and overburdened. She might cut out some irritation by simply making her decisions and not even talking about them; buying the new cooker and matter-of-factly assuming it will be paid for, having the builder in about the damp rot without consulting her husband. This kind of treatment will often surprise a lazy man into wanting to be asked his opinion; in which case he can be manoeuvred into decisive action. If it merely minimises irritation, however, it has done something.

When we marry we accept a partner's shortcomings and inconsistencies; and by laughing at them a little, refusing ever to let them build up into great coral reefs of smouldering resentment, we gradually even come to cherish them.

My husband, recently retired, has very willingly taken over quite a few of the chores I regarded as my share of our joint home-life when we were both full-time employees. Mostly I'm delighted, but just sometimes – very occasionally – I feel a ghost of jealousy, of usurped authority. I've lost a lot of tiring duties, but also a corner of my kingdom.

Let any wife who hankers after being given her orders ask herself – and answer honestly – would she *really* like just to be obedient?

'Prayer for the Day' is broadcast an hour earlier than 'Thought', and is intended to merge gently with the awakening of the day.

'Keep it simple', urged my first producer, Father Pat McEnroe, 'no one's looking for theology or psychology at 6.45 – just the spiritual equivalent of a nice cup of tea.'

All the same it had to be very good tea to please him – nothing wishy-washy or half-brewed.

A Funny Thing Happened . . .

Against Quarrels

I was getting dressed after a swim when I heard the two voices.

'I think these family quarrels are terrible things,' said the first sadly.'Sometimes they go on for years and years, and all about some little thing.'

'Yes they do,' said the second voice, with a certain satisfaction. 'Take me and my elder sister, Flo, for instance. She told my husband, when I was expecting my youngest, that I was neglecting our Mum. As if I would – I was very poorly at the time and the doctor had told me I mustn't go out or I might lose the baby. When Bert told me what she'd said, that finished it. I haven't spoken to her for twenty-three years.'

'Well, I never,' said the first voice feebly. I sympathised with her; I couldn't have thought of any other comment either.

To me that kind of quarrel is a horrible thing, to be avoided, if not quite at all costs, by every possible honest means, for what is the good of it?

When two dogs in the street circle each other, snarling and growling, stiff with aggression, their owners can take them by the tail and pull them apart, but you can't order an irate mother back to her kennel, or give your uncle a sharp tap on the nose to teach him better manners. Human beings can only discipline themselves; outsiders have to listen to the sounds of their anger and, if invited, may try to coax the battlers to see common sense.

The trouble is, though, that it's not everyone who regards it as common sense to try to avoid quarrels.

Some of us, and I don't think they have much choice in the matter, are born to trouble as the sparks fly upwards, and really revel in fights. They like to wound, if only with the tongue, and are prepared to take any rough words thrown back at them – woe betide any passer-by who tries to intervene.

Others enjoy the slow burn. Like Flo's sister, they take a sort of corrosive pleasure in cherishing insult, like some noxious plant, until it has grown into a giant tree overshadowing all their lives. Take this away from them, and what would their imagination have to work on?

Honestly I don't know. For me it's always better to apologise fast, even if I'm not quite sure what my offence may have been. This should clear away hostility, making it plain that I didn't mean to offend and am anxious to put right any error or misunderstanding. While angry feelings still prevail, one never gets anywhere, only the anger can be heard and the desire to give pain. But when this goes, the row can be settled and one can get on with life again. Time is so full of things that are more enjoyable than conflict – swimming, for instance, as I had been when I heard the two voices, and having a cup of hot soup afterwards and reflecting that one may meet the mystery of human nature anywhere.

Lord, in whose understanding we all have our being, teach us to understand each other better, so that those who seem most invulnerable to tenderness may never go unloved or unwanted in your world.

Concerning Beauty

The other morning I was putting myself through what the women's magazines would regard as a most important beauty routine. With a small warm tin of melted wax in one hand and a little wooden spatula in the other, I was painfully tearing out my beard and moustache by the roots – and really quite enjoying it – although if anyone had held me captive and subjected me to the same suffering against my will, I'd have screamed the house down and claimed I was being tortured.

What is it about vanity that makes us so ready to suffer so much in its name? In hot climates men still wear heavy, skin-tight service uniforms on formal occasions, and judges don full-bottomed wigs to appear more dignified and stately. Women diet to the bone nowadays and used to wear crippling corsets to look slim or emphasise curves, high heels give stature to both sexes, shoulder pads imply masculinity, expensive and painful cosmetic surgery is endured by men and women alike. We certainly do crave to look good outwardly.

And there is, of course, a good side to vanity. The person who takes pains to be clean, groomed, nicely dressed is showing that he or she respects the other people in the street and is doing his or her best to look seemly for them. The deliberately scruffy and unkempt are signalling that they don't care a fig for anyone; the ones who are scruffy through no fault of their own are asking for help as loudly as if they were screaming. Oh yes, there's good in vanity.

But why don't we care as much about being beautiful inwardly as outwardly: How often does a woman ask the price of having her ideals rather than her face lifted? Or a man buy a book on a diet of spirituality rather than a tot of spirits? How many of us go to humility classes as well as keep fit, or take a course of charity instead of regularly attending the slimming club?

Well, some are blameless, needless to say. They attend Bible classes and pray regularly on their knees. Most of us, though, are embarrassed by our souls, just as we'd be embarrassed by walking about openly in ugly, dirty garments with filthy hair and face. If these inner components of ours are disgraceful, better disown them altogether, claim they don't exist and laugh at the people who say they are the most important factor in our lives, and that we are as much responsible for them as we are for our waistline or the pimples on our faces.

The trouble with a soul is that no one can see it, or even define it.

But we can all recognise soullessness – the cold, selfish indifference to others, the callous pursuit of money or power regardless of everything else, the quality which demeans life. No sensible person could desire to be soulless, because it involves becoming entirely unlovable and without love life is hell.

So how do we beautify our souls? How do we become inwardly generous, understanding, encouraging, tolerant, secure, so that the attractiveness within quite outshines any outward deformity? Well, we can always go to a specialist (as one might go to a beauty specialist), and if you are a churchgoer, your priest of course can help. If, like me, you aren't a churchgoer, then you have to go direct to the top.

Dear Lord, in this world of illusion and appearances, give me your own cleansing and renewal so that I may be aware of the inner beauty of human life and eventually, perhaps, become a part of it.

Things that Can't be Helped

When we first went to live in the country well over thirty years ago, someone told me a sad old farming story.

Maybe you didn't know (as I didn't at the time) that tame ducks make shocking mothers, and ducks' eggs are nearly always hatched out by chickens. One motherly hen had always been given duck eggs to hatch, then one day, for some unknown reason, she was promoted to a clutch of eleven of her own, and patiently brooded over them until the glad moment when the little fluffy nestlings emerged.

As usual she was pleased and most attentive, and at first all went well. The newcomers piped and cheeped and pecked about with lively interest, but then, as time went on, Mum got very worried. These youngsters weren't behaving according to plan. She did her best with kindly persuasion and rather bossy clucks, but was still ignored. Finally she felt they must be disciplined for their own good; she knew how chicks should behave.

So with stern authority, she rounded them up and drove them into the farmyard pond where every other brood she'd ever known had always, at that stage in their lives, insisted on swimming. Alas, alas. She was frantic, but there were no survivors.

Sheer stupidity, you may say. Yes, but it wasn't her fault, it really wasn't.

And it seems to me that many of the disasters that occur really aren't anyone's fault, and often the worst wrong about a tragedy is the time and anger wasted hounding down someone we can blame for it – someone no more really guilty than the old ritual scapegoat, driven out into the desert laden with sins he'd never committed.

But why, I wonder, are some of us so keen to believe that we humans are responsible for everything – from daybreak and volcanic eruptions to the death of a baby chick? It's true, of course, that we are to blame for a good deal, and that with more care and intelligence we might avoid more catastrophes. But there are always even more, that we could not possibly foresee, let alone prevent, try as we might – the heartache and the thousand natural shocks that flesh is heir to, as Shakespeare put it. There is a dark side to every life, as inescapable as the bright and beautiful.

So what must we do? Blame the Lord and hate Him for making us miserable some of the time, and always setting us insoluble riddles about justice and mercy? Maybe it is only when circumstances make us hate Him that some of us ever give Him a thought: we don't notice the ordinary, homespun goodness which makes up the majority of experience. Working, eating and drinking, making love, bringing up children, studying, trying to get rich, enjoying ourselves – most of life is wholesome and satisfying, and taken completely for granted, and we think we manufacture it ourselves.

Then suddenly, crash! Abruptly we know we are not in control, that our schemes are paperthin, that there is an unknown authority, unpredictable, awesome, directing us. We have never been captain of our soul or master of our fate after all.

Disturbing? Yes, but is it so bad to recognise that we are not totally at the mercy of our own kind, that there is a greater power than man's whose plans for us include death and rebirth, heaven and hell?

Dear Lord, who moves in a mysterious way, give us courage and sense to take life from you as it is dealt to us, rough and smooth, confident that in your possession we are eternally safe.

On Guilt

It gave me a nasty shock to see the policeman standing there when I came back with my shopping.

'Excuse me, madam,' he said. 'Is this your car?'

'Yes,' I said, then in a rush of self-defence, 'but I'm sure I haven't been here for more than fifteen minutes, and it's the right side of the road . . . '

'Yes,' he said, 'but your road fund licence is two months out of date.'

My mouth must have dropped open: there was the evidence of guilt staring us both in the face. 'Good heavens,' I said helplessly, 'you're quite right. I've forgotten all about it.'

'You haven't just applied for it, or got it at home and not displayed it?' he was tempting me with excuses. 'No,' I said, 'it's just plain carelessness. I've got a driving licence and insurance certificate if you want to see them . . . '

'No,' he said, 'that's not necessary, I don't doubt your word. But attend to that licence at once, because you're driving illegally until you do. Good morning.' And off he went, leaving me weak at the knees with the rush of relief that comes of being forgiven when you know you deserve the opposite.

It made me think again about forgiveness, that little episode.

You see on the whole I don't like it.

If anyone takes a forgiving tone to me about something I've done, I tend to get resentful. I can think of excellent reasons for my behaviour which the forgiver simply hasn't grasped. I'm not in the wrong really – misunderstood and rather ill-used, if anything. I know others are like me too – I remember a wife whose letter to me said: 'I forgave him for being unfaithful to me, but he wasn't grateful. He seemed to think I was to blame for being in the right.'

I had great sympathy with her, but I also knew how her husband felt. It was partly her aggravating faultlessness which had driven him to seek company more on his own moral level. She made him feel inferior; he couldn't forgive her for that, so they were at deadlock.

So maybe the first ingredient of forgiveness is mutual understanding; my policeman could understand and be merciful to carelessness, when he wouldn't have had much patience with excuses. I understood that I hadn't a leg to stand on and was grateful and more impressed by clemency than I would have been by punishment.

But what about those other things that I leave undone when they ought to be done, or do when they should be left alone?

Well, of course, no one escapes the everyday consequences of their actions; if I let fat boil over while I read the paper, I risk burning the kitchen curtains; if I pick a quarrel, I must expect to be called names. But I am allowed to go on being a heedless fool and the Lord keeps patiently on forgiving me in the hope, I suppose, that one day I'll learn more sense.

A shock like the policeman leads to slight improvement; making a diary note about the date of the next car licence, for instance, reminded me that I'd almost forgotten an important birthday and the promise I'd made to visit an old lady who likes a bit of a chat. Also I was reminded of things I should be grateful for – health, a roof over my head, work I enjoy, the great blessings which are taken for granted until some tiny beam of enlightenment makes me realise how rare they are and how remiss I am not to be eternally thanking God for them.

Perhaps it is this basic ingratitude which produces guilt feelings in so many of us which we can't explain, except for the wrong reasons. Devoted parents, for instance, who feel guilty about the way they bring up their children; older children who feel guilty at not giving more attention to their cosseted aged parents; people, in fact, who can never enjoy anything properly because they are constantly aware of those in the world with nothing apparently to enjoy. When we have a sense of nagging worry, a feeling we have forgotten something very important, it may be the road fund licence – but it's more likely to be a prayer of thankfulness to our forgiving Lord.

Dear God, who made us and understands us, show us our faults and teach us to repent of them with all our hearts so that we may be truly forgiven.

On Loving and Liking

The other morning I woke up from a dream about my grandmother who lived to be ninety-six; a formidable old cockney, born in 1865, who could remember the Dover coach leaving the Old Kent Road on a winter's night, torches flaring, passengers bundled in rugs sitting on the box outside, the horses' breath steaming on the cold air.

'We was brought up 'ard in those days,' she would say grimly. 'Different to you soft lot.' She admired industry, determination, watchfulness; the need to survive had made her a good fighter, so she took offence easily and enjoyed quarrelling. I'm afraid nobody liked her for long, and she didn't bother with liking them.

With three daughters to care for (twenty-one white pinafores in every week's wash), and eight carthorses in Grandpa's stables to feed and water, she was gloriously indispensable and could happily despise the rest of the world. She told off all her neighbours and relations, and eventually saw them die or fade out of her life. In the end, there were just her grandchildren, and being the female of those, I became mainly responsible for her welfare.

She'd been at odds with me, of course, for years. She hated my job, criticised my husband, made trouble with our friends when she was living with us and one day I realised with horror that I was beginning to hate her. But this was unthinkable because she depended on me.

So during a shouting match – she was stone-deaf, nearly – I heard myself blurt out, at the top of my voice: 'You can be as nasty as you like, Gran, but you can't drive me away. I'll always come back. I love you, and I'm going to look after you, so put that in your pipe and smoke it.'

I didn't, of course, feel the least bit loving; I was angry. But the word love shocked both of us into silence; it didn't normally come into family rows and I'd never until then considered what it really meant, and what sort of action it entailed.

How, after all, do you love someone you don't like, how can you act lovingly towards them? Plug on, obviously, doing whatever sort of thing seems likely to be good for them in the face of contemptuous opposition. But what sort of person could be capable of such a thankless task? A saint?

No, you needn't be a saint. I thought of a mother with a young baby. He keeps her awake at nights for weeks on end, fights her when she tries to attend to his needs, is sick all down her only good frock, fills her with exasperation. But does she walk out on him, bitterly offended at his ingratitude? Of course not. All she asks is that he shall flourish and she be allowed to go on being his slave, because she truly loves him. She may not *like* him; he's too young yet for her to know, but she isn't worrying about it.

So I hadn't to worry about disliking my grandmother, and as a matter of fact, I never did worry about that any more. I found that once I didn't expect her to change or soften towards me, I could take quite a lot of her ill-humour as a joke, and I found a lot more sympathy for the many aches and pains she suffered as a result of old age (and was very brave about, I may say).

And once I expected no improvement in her, it seemed that she did become slightly more mellow and less contemptuous. Indeed, one Christmas she actually thanked my brother for the present he gave her instead of saying as usual, 'What did you want to waste your money on that for?'

I glimpsed that the spirit of love, which is God, is probably basically this endless, powerful, unoffendable benevolence poured out in a stream for us all, and largely unfelt because as human beings we either can't or won't know what is good for us. But however much we deny it or ignore it, or are insensitive to it, God's love is irresistible because it is the life force itself.

Dear Lord, teach us more about our true nature and its needs, and your own nature which is love itself. Give us the willingness to live for others so that the Holy Spirit may flow through us freely and bring healing and hope to many more than ourselves.

Devil's Eye View

Walking to work along one of London's great shopping streets, I saw a woman coming towards me. She was stumping along, feet turned slightly outwards, head hunched between her shoulders, weighed down with a bag in either hand and on her face the expression of one carrying all the world's woes. 'My heavens,' I said to myself, 'what a sight she is. Pity the poor chap who sits opposite that face every morning at breakfast.'

And then I froze. Because the woman was me and the face was mine; I'd come right into the range of a mirror some wicked shop had hung in its window.

It was a nasty facer, that one. It's all very well for Robert Burns to have written, 'Oh, wad some power the giftie gie us To see ourselves as ithers see us' (pardon my Gaelic) but why didn't he add: 'And please, dear Lord, do not omit the power to stand the shock of it.'

For to catch a glimpse of oneself all unawares is to experience, just for a second, a sort of devil's eye view; all the weakness, force and folly we can read in the countenance of others we realise is all too plain in our own.

I saw, for instance, what I always hope I conceal, a gloominess and pessimism which are quite unjustified, since I know I am a lucky person. I saw also a grimness I hadn't suspected; can I really be so dour and determined a character? And I was reminded of how disgracefully I move – slumped forward, flat-footed, as if my shopping bags were really heavy instead of being more or less empty except for a couple of books.

I thought how heroic my husband must be to have put up with this wreck of a woman for nearly forty years, and when I got home that night I threw my arms round him and said, 'Darling, you are wonderful!' with such fervour that he was taken aback. In great puzzlement he patted me gently and said,'There, there, darling, I love you', as if I had been about six years old and needed comforting, which of course I did. The merciful realisation that however awful I seemed to myself there was another human being who could put up with me was like receiving a very rich gift indeed.

I think it is when this gift is lacking, when a human partner or comforter dies or leaves or has never been found that really bitter loneliness may move into a personality and fill every day with fear and resentment. To suspect we are unlovable is the worst kind of suspicion, and when we begin to feel it we most desperately need a reminder that God never leaves us, is probably nearest when we feel most desolate and is attracting us most strongly towards asking for His help – because only when we acknowledge our need for it can we recognise that help.

In a lifetime of trying to be helpful to people in trouble I have felt that the admission of the need for help is the greatest step we ever make towards happiness, and almost the only action we can perform out of our own freewill and not through our programming as children of our parents and products of our society.

While we say: 'No one can help me, I'm beyond the aid of God or man, and I don't believe in prayer because none of my prayers ever gets answered,' then we are truly unhelpable, too proud to consider that anyone can be wiser or more powerful than ourselves. But when the cry changes to: 'It's no good, I can't cope, I need help' – it won't matter that you don't even know you are praying. You will have grasped your own insufficiency and the help of God will be given.

It may not be at all the help you expected or hoped for, but there will be some task to do, some action to perform (like telling your partner he's wonderful) which will lift you out of despair into some more tolerable situation.

Lord, who loves us as we really are, give each of us a sense of your nearness and authority, so that however hopeless we feel ourselves to be we are always reminded of your loving presence and understanding.

'Pause for Thought' belongs to Radio 2, the DJ's kingdom of the early morning when people are getting up, thinking about everything but deeply serious concerns, and yet somehow in need of a bit of solid spiritual nourishment as well as the cereal and the hastily-swallowed cuppa.

Here are a set of four broadcasts I made when I first retired from being an agony auntie, knowing that the people who had written to me for help on a woman's magazine would be sure to be among my listeners.

Secret Session

Guilty Secrets

A lot of my problems when I was Evelyn Home were about secrets, especially guilty secrets, which apart from tight shoes, are about the most uncomfortable thing in the world to have. Take Sue's case.

She was twenty-two, engaged to her ideal man – we'll call him Gerald. He loved her as much as she loved him, and when they got engaged she should have been, as they say, the happiest girl in the world but she wasn't. She found, you see, that she had an awful urge to tell Gerald all about a couple of affairs she'd had before she met him. The weight on her conscience seemed like a lorry-load of concrete. If only she could tell him and be forgiven.

Then, she felt, she really could be the happiest girl in the world, but he just didn't seem to want to know the details of her past, he kept saying all he was interested in were her feelings *now*.

Sue couldn't rest, and one day she burst out with a full dramatic confession, but instead of being sympathetic, understanding and forgiving, Gerald was mad with her. He said it was like having a lot of dirty water poured over him, and why couldn't she keep her guilt to herself? He hadn't burdened her with his sins, he pointed out, he wasn't proud of past mistakes. He reckoned it was his job to make good and put them behind him, not force her to know the bad side of him, which he hoped he was growing out of, largely through meeting her and learning what love really was.

And while she stood, dumb and dismayed, he said he thought they'd better part for a few months and see if they still cared for each other after that.

She wrote to me in a panic at that point. She'd always believed, you see, that if you told the truth you were bound to be forgiven. But just telling the truth I suppose isn't enough. There's nearly always need for a pause for thought about the other person before trying to get yourself out of an uncomfortable situation, and easing your own conscience at the expense of his peace of mind.

Sometimes the punishment for a guilty secret is just having to put up with it, in the silent knowledge that you're an ordinary, sinful sort of person, no better than anybody else, with a skeleton in your cupboard too. It's not fair to try to push it on to somebody else unless, of course, you have faith and can share it with the Lord. He always forgives, unlike even the most loving human being.

Other People's Secrets

Of course, everyone really knows the basic rules about secrets; if possible never have any; if you must have a few, keep them to yourself. And if by chance you uncover somebody else's just cover them up again fast, unless – well unless it would be absolutely criminal to keep them dark. But I'm not talking about colossal secrets, witnessing a murder, for instance. I'm aiming at little secrets which matter enormously to those who have a different idea of what is shameful from yours.

I've never forgotten, for instance, that years ago I was taught piano by the father of a family all living in a rather small flat, four large-sized grown-ups and a huge piano in the Music Room where we pupils worked. When we weren't actually at the piano, we sat on a couch with our manuscript books, but one day another little girl at class with me asked if she could sit up to the table to write, then she said the terrible words, 'I'm not very comfortable working on the bed.'

Suddenly the room seemed full of thunder. Our teacher was furious. Then he said, 'Go away, Peggy, I want to talk to Nancy.' Well of course after the lesson I rushed round to Nancy's to hear what had happened. 'He said I was a horrible little girl,' Nancy said. 'He knew his son had to sleep in the Music Room, but did I have to shout it out in front of you and make him ashamed of being poor?'

I was astonished, I hadn't known the couch was a bed, but did it matter if it was? And Mr X wasn't really poor, he wasn't in rags or starving, which was my idea of poverty at the age of ten, and he played the piano beautifully, he must be quite a high-up person.

It was my first experience of other people's secrets which are often connected with rather silly snobberies, but which matter terribly to them. And today I think these are secrets to respect and not look down on. I know some women who are ashamed to be seen cashing fourpence-off type vouchers in the supermarket, and we all know Senior Citizens who don't care to collect their pension from the local Post Office where everyone will see them: I'm sorry they feel that way, but – well I have my little secrets too, which I'm not telling. And I won't give you away either, even if I actually see you furtively taking the printed wrapping off that cake you said you made yourself.

Secret Love

Have you ever had that sudden love at first sight feeling at a party? You know what I mean, the entangling glance which holds like a spell.

Well, if you're married to somebody else, that's the moment for you to say nothing. If only people could do that, so much misery would be avoided. But all too often temptation wins. Here's a bit from a letter:

'Neither of us meant to say it, but somehow we got talking about love, and after that we couldn't struggle any more.' That was a woman describing the first thrilling moments of an affair which wrecked two previously happy families.

She insisted that she hadn't meant to be unfaithful, and I believe her, but there was a moment when she could have kept the secret of his attraction for her, then maybe the tragedy might not have happened.

After all, we all have tumultuous feelings, I have plenty. I'd hate to confess the number of times I've fallen helplessly in love across a crowded room. It's like a great wave, but waves recede and your brain and your breath come back again.

I remember then how much I enjoy my marriage, and how I couldn't be a traitor to my husband, who's put up with me so long, then I'm all right again.

And I don't fall out of love immediately, I still think what a wonderful man, but if we do get to talk, I keep it casual and don't respond to any sort of personal approach. Oh yes, passes are made, even at people of my age. But any man who isn't as dumb as a fish picks up the message at once, he knows as I know that though for a second or two you were as one, possible lovers, the idea has been totally rejected. You have to believe, as I do, that genuine love can never be harmful, because it wants only the good of the beloved – certainly not to wreck his life.

So if you have ever wished, even for a second, that you could be someone's lover, someone who belongs to someone else, you can pray from the heart that love, not your love, but love itself, straight from the fountain head may be given to him or her. Then the pain of the secret is eased in the joy of being able to give something better than yourself.

Secret Sorrow

Forgive me if I pause for thought about something sad, and often kept secret, I mean sorrow. The sorrow which people feel who have lost a husband or wife or child or parent, or someone specially dear, which they feel they must hide.

'I've been in the depths long enough,' one widow told me. 'I feel just as bad but I can tell that people are getting fed-up with me. So now I just say I'm OK and try to shut the grief away.' But she'd only been widowed three months. This is no time at all in which to get over a companionship of twenty happy years, it's expecting a severe wound to heal in hours rather than weeks.

I think as a people we're too ashamed of mourning. We hate others to see us with tears in our eyes, or losing control of our voice. We want to be thought brave and independent, not silly cry-babies. But crying is a help in grief, even for men who grow up being taught never to show their feelings, and there are plenty who are still brought up on this unimaginative old formula.

To weep is to release the despair and misery which may otherwise turn inward and can actually become a sickness. 'If I talk about it, I shall break down,' a man told me after his wife's death. I didn't mind his breaking down. He was the sufferer, it did me no harm to sympathise with his tears for his wife. It touched me to the quick, but that's no hardship.

There really is no need to make a secret of grief, unless perhaps one is mourning for a secret lover, a person one had no real right to love, then the worst part of the pain is having to conceal natural acute sorrow. But the person who goes into an illicit affair knows the consequences.

If you've loved anybody, you're bound to mourn their death. Only those who have never meant anything to you can die and leave you untouched. People, other people, are the best healers of grief, but they can't function unless they know you're grieving. So I beg anyone in secret agony of loss, don't be too proud to let your friends know how you feel; we all want to help you to recover.

There are special occasions in the Christian year which seem to call for prayers of their own – occasions which mean something to the ordinary unthinking Christian as well as the seasoned churchgoer. Here are two sets of festival prayers – one for the week leading up to Whitsun and Pentecost, one for Christmas, times when heaven should feel close to earth.

Points of No Return

Awareness

It was while I was searching ruefully for the few strands of brown hair left in my grey thatch that I found myself thinking of all the points of no return an ordinary life holds. When, I wondered, had I last looked for grey among the brown? And at once recalled that between old age and youth there must have been a million other endings, some unnoticeable, others marked forever.

The earliest most significant for me, perhaps, was the birth of my first young brother. I was five, the family was over-loaded with females and the outsize welcome which greeted this squalling red infant, just because it was male, made me realise that life was never going to be the same again.

I didn't know, of course, that the blackness which over-whelmed me was jealousy and shameful; all I knew was that I had been some sort of queen in the home, and now I was nothing – compared to King Baby Brother.

There would be no return to the throne; I became a half-pint cauldron of boiling hatred and resentment. I believe I learned a good deal about hell between five and fifteen.

For many years, long after I'd grown to love both my brothers, this seemed nothing but a warping, distorting experience I could well have done without. Then gradually I began to see another aspect of it.

You know how a potter making, say, a jug, starts by giving the inert clay one or two very hard blows, almost karate chops, which he knows are necessary if it is ever to attain its final, planned shape?

Well, I think that first blow which knocked me out of smug babyhood was no accident. It was the beginning of thought and puzzlement, of asking the kind of questions which don't, I think, usually enter the mind at the age of six – in fact, it made me start considering what I was, why I was and who had made me.

There wasn't much fun in these primary lessons in self-awareness. Perhaps one of the reasons I learned to read so early was to escape the daily diet of having to be a little girl who ought to be happy to have a dear little brother – but was just the opposite. In stories one can retreat into some other character's life and temporarily forget one's own.

But once awake to the riddle of creation, it can't be ignored for long. God, they said to me at Sunday School, is good and loving, and wants everyone to be happy. I didn't just doubt this; I knew it was rot.

Life was a round dark hole in which I was a very uncomfortable square peg; people were sometimes kind and loving, but God had made me someone I didn't want to be. I was accused of ingratitude when I disliked it. But what could you expect when you learned what God had done to his own son? Let him be crucified. So what was he likely to do for me?

You might imagine that such a point of no return might have meant a cynical, scornful, hopeless approach to maturity. Yet it turned out to be a journey into faith, hope and love, accepting granite reality, the inevitability of pain, and seeing that in everlasting life there must be a place where suffering and ecstasy can be separately experienced, and where time seems real, not simply a method of measuring human existence.

Dear God, give us alertness to recognise your promptings and persistence to follow them; wake us up when we would rather sleep and let us distrust coming to conclusions in your never-ending kingdom.

The Start of a Voyage

Hanging wet towels on the line, I was thinking again about life's points of no return, and wondering why the subject sounds so doleful, because, of course, it needn't be. Many of these last occasions, maybe most of them, are really causes for rejoicing not regrets.

Take a nice simple milestone, never passed by some. Every

Thursday evening after work, my father would take me with him to the swimming baths. He'd give me a few minutes' instruction, hand under my chin, then leave me to sink by myself while he swam a manly trudgen stroke up and down the lengths.

I'd bob around in the tepid waves, cling on to the rail, or push off from the shallow end steps then find I was walking. But one famous Thursday I pushed off from the steps, my feet rose, I struck out – and I didn't sink. Suddenly I could swim, and very triumphant, I travelled home on the bus. Then a terrible thought struck me.

'Will I have forgotten how to do it next time?' I asked.

'No, you'll never forget how to swim,' said Dad confidently. And that was the beginning of years of pleasure afloat, culminating in that moment when I hung our wet towels on the line, a point of no return to be thankful for.

A similar glad shock is learning to ride a bicycle. Somewhere in your body, unless you're unlucky, is something that knows how to balance on two narrow wheels, and once you've gained confidence in it, the skill is unfailing. I tried again the other day, after twenty years, and sure enough I could still ride, though I had to fall off when I wanted to dismount.

But there is an even more remarkable point of no return which seems to involve physical, mental and spiritual qualities.

'In the beginning,' says St John's gospel, 'was the Word.' And this is supposed to mean divine wisdom, not the development from grunts and squeals to expressive language.

But when I think of this phrase, I feel it wasn't so much neat wisdom that St John was trying to describe, but an immediate experience men have of God. The Word was a method the Almighty had chosen for communicating with men which enabled their earthbound minds to understand His message.

It is a way for us to reach Him; also a way in which we can reach each other through our mutual knowledge of Him. It is very like, to me, learning to read.

I remember this as a small miracle. One day I was plodding away at my Infants' Primer, mouthing 'K A T – cat', and next day, literally, I could read the little book at a sitting, taking in whole sentences at a gulp. Newspapers, posters, notices, everything printed meant something at last; I had longed to be able to see elves and fairies, but now I could live in a world of fairy tales. It was like the light being switched on in a dark room.

And I think recognising the word of God is just such a light; a point of no return to ignorance, even if at times ignorance seemed to be bliss. Once one knows that the wisdom is there, available, that all the truth within man's comprehension is communicable – not the unspeakable wisdom of omnipotence which men cannot acquire, but the speakable wisdom which can be shared with others in God – then the point of no return becomes the start of the voyage.

Dear Lord, who has given us the curiosity to question and the audacity to explore, give us also the wits to recognise truth when we find it and the humility to realise that we would never have sought for it, but for your promptings.

To Live as He Lived

Today – Ascension Day – always takes me back in mind to the dusty old Mission Hall in which I went to Sunday School and which, I sometimes fear, turned me partly into a heathen for ever. But it did give me some pictures as bookmarks for my Bible, and a particularly vivid one showed Jesus in billowing white robes being escorted up into the sky by two angels in rather less billowing robes, and the shadowy face of God waiting in a cloud to receive him. At the bottom of the picture were the upturned faces of the Apostles; looking sad as well as awed, because this was the unique point of no return, the day when they knew that their Master would never be with them bodily again.

But if ever a point of no return was the true start of a great adventure, this was.

I once heard Archbishop Ramsay say that though scholars and Christians held differing views on many aspects of the Jesus story, they all agreed that Christ died and that after his death arose a movement bearing his name which was so aflame with love and self-sacrifice that it had transformed the world.

But has it? Isn't the world the same now as it's always been, shot through with greed and malice; so that it can crucify a man for the awful crime of suggesting that we might love God and our neighbour as ourselves and that those in authority should regard themselves as servants of their people?

Yes, of course it is the same now – there are always people to say that loving your neighbour as yourself is an unrealisable ideal; there are also plenty in authority who may begin by thinking themselves public servants, but quite soon forget everything but the thrill of giving orders.

But here is a bit of transformation; no one can assert now that the right way to live our lives is unknown, hidden in mystery. No one can pretend that a ruler should run a country entirely for his own benefit, or that it's quite proper to loathe your neighbour. Of course Christ's commandments weren't new when he uttered them, but what made them new was that He actually practised what He preached.

He didn't just say that it was blessed to be poor; he *was* poor and never wasted a second trying to do better for himself. He didn't just speak piously about bringing up children, he welcomed them around him and told stories they could understand rather than boring them with theological arguments.

He didn't just wish people all the good in the world, he cured their ills, mental as well as physical, assured them that their sins were forgiven and now they could go and get on with life. He insisted on the living spirit, not the dead letter of religious law.

Then, having talked with his followers for the last time, he was taken up into heaven. But He promised to send His comforter to inspire them, and sure enough, at Pentecost our Whit Sunday, Christianity began. It began with words and the sudden power of strangers to understand each other, it gave new confidence to those who felt drowned in the sorrows of life and a new sense of balance between the forces of destruction and eternal creation.

As nations, we haven't dared try the new wisdom which Christ lived by; but some individuals have done their best to live as He lived, so lovingly, that death could not hold Him. We know now that it can be done, and we have been saved from despair. So let us thank God for Him this morning, and for His shining example.

Christmas Forever

Another Year

Long before there were angels singing in the skies, Santa Claus coming down chimneys with sacks of presents or even the Christ Child lying in his manger, we had a festival here in Britain at Christmas time.

Not even the archaeologists know quite how it was ordered, what Stone Age carols they sang or how the prayers went, but the gratitude to heaven in the hearts of the congregation wrapped in their draughty animal skins was perhaps even more sincere than that ascending from the innumerable churches of today's civilised world.

Why were those early men thanking God?

Because for a very long time their hill watchers would have been measuring the slow shortening of the days, marking the dawn's appearance later and later, the sun hidden in clouds of fog, and the absolute darkness of night falling like an avalanche earlier and earlier.

With an absence of sun went an absence of food to be gleaned from plant-life, and the increased savagery and shyness of the wild animals who shared man's homelands. It became harder and harder to survive as the days diminished, and the fear of death would have been very real indeed among those far-off ancestors of ours.

Then one morning it would appear to the most acutely aware of the watchers that the sun had arrived a very little earlier, and had lingered a fraction longer at dusk. How exactly they measured time and light we can't tell, but in a day or two more, it would have become clear that the life-giving majesty in the sky was not dying, but returning from a long journey – quite certainly returning. And with his return would come eventually warmth and melting snow and the fullness of spring.

Looking at prehistoric homes, I've tried hard to imagine the sense of relief around the fires in the caves and the hearths of the small round stone houses. The promise of brightness to come must have cured many a case of depression and given renewed energy to the tired limbs of hunters and food-gatherers. Light was coming back; they must have sung and perhaps danced and made up their minds to endure and feel the sun's warmth once more.

I believe that ancient thankfulness for the relenting of winter is still giving underlying strength to our Christian celebrations today, in the midst of the same old darkness and discouragement.

We no longer credit the sun with the power to be offended and hide his face as a punishment for our impudence.

In fact we say: 'How silly they were to worship a planet in the sky, whatever good could that do them?' But I think they had more wits than we realise. Behind the heavenly bodies and the wind, water, fire and earth that were the original elements they felt the existence of an awesome power pervading all nature, which could nonetheless be reached by humility and obedience to its will.

To propitiate this power, to acknowledge its superiority seemed to them common sense. Although they could not read, the truth of that well-known Bible phrase, 'The fear of the Lord is the beginning of wisdom' lay at the roots of their actions.

Nowadays many of us would think ourselves fools if we thanked God for the sun's return this Christmas. We can, after all, harness light at any moment of the day or night for our own uses, however trivial.

But shouldn't we still be thankful, even if the gift is one of the oldest presented by the Creator to the world and its inhabitants?

Dear God, don't let us forget that this splendid feast of Christmas commemorates not only a holy birth, but that it is also the genesis of another living year. Give us light to see through the extravagances and follies of the holiday to the natural blessing which, whether we realise it or not, we are surely celebrating.

Warmth and Light

This is a great season for memories, but I am trying to cast my mind back to an age before living memory, when Christmas was not called Christmas for Christ had not yet been born. Men and women, though, in this part of the world were already celebrating a festival of light at this time of the year in honour of the return of the sun after the shortest day.

No one, though, could have celebrated anything in the untempered cold, and one of the oldest Greek myths tells us that a man stole fire from heaven originally, and was punished horribly by the gods for his effrontery.

What stories men and women told here to account for the fires in their caves and stone huts we have no way of knowing, but one of their habitual ways of revering nature was to build great fires, and one of their unceasing customs would have been diligently to tend the family fire because in the dark days it was their only defence against freezing.

Initially the fire was also the only source of light other than the sun, and families around the flames must have loved it when there was plenty of wood to burn and faces would be lit up almost as if it were day.

It would have been much later, when there was thread to make a wick and oil or fat to float it in, that an alternative source to firelight was found. The first candles and lamps glimmered through the chinks in rough walls and the kingdom of darkness retreated another step backwards in time.

The winter solstice festival then must have seemed a comparative blaze of light, with kindling stacked high to roast the meat which would not keep, and lamps proudly ensconced in walls. People replete with food, bemused with the dazzle and relaxed in warmth must have thanked their gods for a respite from winter – a short spell of comfort to remember when the frost and snow clamped down again and game was sparse and nothing to eat could be found in or on the earth.

Even in my childhood there was much of that festival of light spirit left in Christmas.

Although gas lamps purred over our dining table, little candles in metal holders were clipped on to the tree, and on

Christmas Eve the gas was turned off to show these small lights bravely burning – they were the true illumination of the holiday.

The candlelight struck a gleam from the odd gold and silver paper chain among those festooning the ceiling, and made the tinsel garlanding the tree glitter like hoar frost. The star on the head of the fairy on the treetop would shine, and so would the gold ribbons on her wand and dress – all the little emblems of Christmas were also emblems of light.

Even the holly and mistletoe, those essential decorations which harked back to nature worship and human gratitude for the evergreen and the plant which could grow without roots in the earth – even those were tied with tinsel which sparkled merrily in candlelight, but hardly showed when the gas was turned up again.

Yet we have never lost the taste for candlelight; its warmth, colour and simplicity are still valued not only in our homes, but also in church at every great religious rejoicing.

So let us thank God this morning for the warmth and light we take for granted as part of everyday existence, but which once must have been seen as wonders and gifts from heaven. And let us not forget those who are still caught in the chains of coldness and darkness, physical or spiritual, and pray for their release.

Outer Light – Inner Light

I have been trying to picture Christmastide before Christ, yet with the love and generosity of the Creator permeating it in the feast of the returning sun, the celebrating of light and warmth which our remotest ancestors observed before a word of history was written.

It was a natural festival, growing out of the cycle of the year, planned to hearten people at the darkest time of the seasons and to make them forget, for a few days, the hardships and struggle of life and set their thoughts running towards a brighter future.

All this ancient survival-worship is too basic to humanity to be extinct, in fact is some ways it has over-developed. The feast which was originally a sensible eating-up of food which would otherwise have gone bad has been replaced by plain gluttony, the merrymaking has degenerated into an orgy and the uniting warmth of the hearth has been lost in the glare of the television screen.

Just as neon tubes dim candles, so does the dazzle of worldly and temporary charity blot out the goodwill which the giving heart extends all the year through, and the sudden highlighting of certain church services – carol singings, present distributions and so on – extinguishes the gentle but penetrating illumination which the birth of Christ should add to the old feast of light at the end of the year.

Godgiven sunlight shows up all outside things, the surface of our world, the animals and fish and birds, the vegetation, the skies and the waters. It has power too to make seeds germinate and plants grow; it can initiate fire, can heal or destroy.

Godgiven inner light, which Christ brought, shows the hidden things, chiefly those within ourselves, the very core of our being. The embodiment of love, He forces us to recognise what a piece of work is a man or woman when measured against perfection. And as the patron of Christmas, His light is still a great deal too searching for many, perhaps most of us.

Mary, the gracious obedient maiden who pondered in her heart what it might mean to be the Mother of God and who accepted that almighty burden, she might have faced the divine light without flinching, but who else?

There was a well-off young man who thought he valued his salvation above all things, but the piercing light of Christ showed that he loved riches more. There were learned men who began by arrogantly asking Him questions, but who ended by ignominiously slinking away. There were people in plenty who were sure He was the Messiah they had been longing to follow, but who saw in the relentless light surrounding Him, that they dared not risk it.

So it is not easy to celebrate the truth-revealing inner light whole-heartedly. Can we welcome the knowledge that we are cowards, selfish, cruel, hypocritical, lazy? Do we want to have to regard our real selves, day in and day out, because this is what that light forces us to do once we have opened the shutters and let it in?

To be honest, I fear it – and yet, dear God, give me the courage to face the truth about my faults and weaknesses and to start cleaning away the grime and dirt I do my best to ignore. At this time when the light of the world comes flooding back to us, give us all the strength to make yet another fresh start and go cheerfully on our way to the beginning of a new year.

The Revd Colin Semper, in charge of BBC World Service Religious Broadcasts, felt that in the year 1978 the Women's World Day of Prayer should be featured in his programme called 'Reflections', which is transmitted in the small hours of the UK morning to the turning earth.

The subject given for the Day of Prayer was 'Community Spirit in Modern Living', and it had been selected by Canadian Christian women.

Reflections

Beginning

Friday of this week is Women's World Day of Prayer and I have been reflecting on the theme chosen by the Christian women of Canada. 'Community Spirit in Modern Living'. It sounds very worthy, a general good thought bound to be shared by all Christian church members, and particularly applicable these days when all over the globe there are wars and the rumours of wars – only nowadays, the rumours are nearly always turned into certainties by the reporters and cameras on the spot.

Now, it seems, we need community spirit as never before – but what is it? What does having it mean? How can we show it?

It's easy to think of it as simply peace. We older western women have seen our lovers and loved ones killed and maimed in war, and to many of us peace is just – not war. It is law and order, a settled regime, lack of violence, everybody obeying the regulations outwardly, no matter what may be seething underneath.

After all, one of the strongest attractions of Christianity for us is that its Founder used violence only against sacrilege, and showed us a Father in Heaven who was love itself. How precious that gospel is to us, with children to bring up, husbands to cherish and our traditional desire for harmony around the family hearth.

But is this longing for peace, I wonder, a kind of selfishness in disguise?

As we pray for more community spirit in our lives, are we really asking for more tolerance and cordiality all round so that our cosy homes and family circles may be kept intact, unthreatened by change?

Are we hoping, secretly, that people who feel so righteously ardent about certain noble aims that they are prepared to die for them will drop their agitation and abandon their ideals so that the rest of us may live on undisturbed in an atmosphere of comfortable, ignoble security?

I trust not, but my conscience isn't at all easy.

Suppose I lived in a warring neighbourhood, black versus white or Protestant versus Catholic (we Christians may talk about loving our enemies, but we often don't try to get on with those who should be our best friends) – well, suppose I lived in that kind of place, would I steadfastly stay there on the battlefield, trying to be actively friendly to both sides? Or, if the chance of escape came, would I take it and go like a rocket?

I wish I could believe I'd be brave, but I'm fairly sure that the only reason I might stick it would be that I had no other choice.

So, on reflection, I know that part of my prayer on Friday for community spirit will have to be for the courage to practise, if need be, that even-handed love of humanity which might create a tiny oasis of goodwill in an area full of fear and malice.

I must avoid just asking to be left in peace; I need to be given the energy to become a peace force, if true community spirit is to grow.

And supposing all of us praying for this good end are given the fervour to be a peace force, will we change society? I doubt it, but we ourselves will change because that is how prayer works.

Consider, for instance, if all women Protestants and Catholics began genuinely to befriend each other and work for each other's good – well, it would be a beginning, wouldn't it?

Love Thy Neighbour

Friday will be Women's World Day of Prayer and I have been reflecting seriously on this year's theme, chosen by Canadian women, which is 'Community Spirit in Modern Living'.

It is very Christian, this theme, and must have sprung from Christ's second commandment, that we should love our neighbour as ourselves. I must have heard the phrase read and preached about a million times, but when I came to think deeply about it I began to sense the profundity within.

First, that neighbour. Christ, an orthodox Jew, would have been taught above all to love and honour his parents, to whom he owed his being. And he would have learned from further religious studies that there is no greater love than that which causes a man to lay down his life for his friend.

He might very justifiably have repeated those two demands to the followers who asked him for a rule of life, but he said nothing about parents or friends.

Instead he went deliberately outside the sacred circle of everyone's nearest and dearest and commanded that we should love our neighbour as we love ourself – and who on earth is our neighbour? Or rather, who on earth isn't our neighbour?

Almost anyone can be. The strangers who moved in yesterday, the gipsies camping on the road verge, the rude noisy set in the flat upstairs, the obvious heathen at the end of the back garden, the vandals smashing the street lamp outside – anyone nigh to you, near to you at the moment, is your neighbour.

Jesus didn't say they had to share your church, your moral standards, your nationality or your way of life. He didn't ask us to be fair to them or give them human rights, he said love them.

Well many of us find it hard to love our relations and we don't have many friends. We don't even love ourselves much, beyond possessing enough instinct of self-preservation to stop us throwing ourselves under the nearest bus. I've always thought that drug addicts, chain smokers, alcoholics can't love themselves or they wouldn't have so strong a death-wish, and I expect Christ was making allowances for the likes of them.

And of course to love is not necessarily to like. Jesus knew that well enough when telling us to love not only our neighbour but our enemy. He wanted us, I think, to face the fact that love is not just a feeling of mutual attraction, not just a feeling at all.

What is it, then, when unwarmed by parental or sexual preference?

I'd say, and this is no original thought, that it is active goodwill. It is genuinely wanting the good of all those who may be your neighbours, wanting it as much as your own, working and praying for it just as you work and pray for the good of your children, your parents or your husband.

But suppose you don't know what is good for your neighbour? Not to worry; you probably don't know what is good for you, though if you were me, you'd have an uneasy suspicion that it might be less self-indulgence and more self-discipline. When I genuinely want someone's good, I pray the sort of prayer which says: 'Lord, who knows what is good for everyone, bless my neighbour, and if there is anything I can do to be helpful to her, show me what it is.'

So with my fellow women in Friday's day of prayer, I shall acknowledge Christ's own commitment to the community spirit which arose through his second commandment to us all – after the first commandment which was to love the Lord our God with all our heart and strength, and all our will.

The Community Spirit

Today is Women's World Day of Prayer whose theme, chosen by Canada, is 'Community Spirit in Modern Living'. Reflecting on it, I have discovered how profoundly serious a theme it is, how it leads straight to the heart of Christianity, may for some lead to the Cross itself.

It is a necessary theme because modern living has taken one of those turns away from a previously cherished ideal – the ideal of the brotherhood of all men – and is now going hell for leather for separation and self-interest.

The break-up, for instance, of the old British Empire has led to the birth of dozens of new states, and in most of these the emergence of rival tribes or groups claiming sovereignty. The old world religions have seen fresh questioning and mutiny against central authority, and the massive old Marxist philosophy has splintered into several more political schools of thought and power.

These partings of the ways have not been happy. States freed from the tyranny of colonialism have plunged into civil war; the conflict between Catholics and Protestants has broken out again very fiercely, also the conflict between Christians and

Moslems, the Holy Land has been the scene throughout history of particularly unholy hatred and cruelty.

I think we women praying today earnestly for the community spirit to flourish will face the fact, being the practical sex, that it is very unlikely the Christian message of peace will reach much further than our own ears. The craving for mastery is too strong for ordinary mortals to resist – what keeps part of our world in an uneasy calm is fear of an atomic war and its results, not any growth of international charity. It will surely only be when the attraction of love is as great as the allure of conquest that community spirit will become the rule wherever human beings exist – and I see no signs of it.

Meanwhile women will do as they always have done, I expect – bring a great and idealistic theme down to earth and find some way of putting it into ordinary everyday practice, just as they transmute the purple and poetry of sexual romance into babies and cooking.

Community spirit for us, the daughters and grannies, will become humdrum neighbourliness, that unemotional word which describes a relationship subtle and complicated, yet outwardly simplicity itself. It doesn't aim for the heights of loving your neighbour as yourself, more's the pity perhaps, but it is much more within the scope of the average female.

Men, I'd say, have the art of being cronies, pals, fellow-members; women's equivalent is to be neighbours. It's a role which I admit a good many of us here in overcrowded urban Britain play pretty coolly. We don't intrude upon our neighbours without being invited unless we see some worrying sign like a cluster of full milk bottles at a back door, which might betoken that a neighbour is ill or injured.

Children quicken up our acquaintance, but even after some years we may not be friends exactly. Yet in emergency we know we may call upon each other for help or consolation – many a cool neighbour has been the first person to comfort a widow in distress, rescue a frightened child from fire or has taken in a whole family after a disaster.

If we can't hope to change society, maybe we can put more drive into our neighbourliness, especially where it goes against the grain – that's when it probably does most good.

Not much to hope for in a world day of prayer? Well, if it changes one no-go area into a community, in some places that would be as good as a miracle.

Finally, here are some reflections on the nature of God Himself, although I use a personal pronoun simply for ease, not because I believe omniscience is masculine – how could it be? Or feminine either, for that matter. No one has seen God – I haven't escaped that quotation, but I believe there is in everyone a gleam of the divine light and the more one looks inwards towards it (not towards one's own self), the more one is encouraged to look.

The World as a Battlefield

'If God did not exist,' wrote the French philosopher, Voltaire, 'it would be necessary to invent Him.'

And suppose that became our peculiar task, what manner of God would we invent? For there is no doubt that at the times nations need a god, and are therefore more likely to turn to him, they usually have just one aspect of his universality in mind. They are in a war situation, fearful of the outcome and desperately need more than human aid – they want divine power on their side.

So, as there seems to have been no time without war, the most popular god for many thousands of years and among all sorts of peoples and races has been the god of victory, the lord of might, who can bring men safely and triumphantly home from battle.

It is not until conflict has died down and the situation stabilised for the time being that the warrior god may cease to be a favourite national deity. He is a great one for crowds and masses, but when the consequences of the fighting narrow down to individual level, the reward of having won is often seen to be little more than bitter responsibilities. Then widows and casualties may be heard murmuring about the emptiness of victory.

Yet some of us are never disillusioned with the idea of conquest. Unconsciously, perhaps, we continue to worship a deity who will help us beat our rivals in life, without considering what kind of god he is bound to be and what kind of person worshipping him will make us.

There's nothing surprising in this. Love of success arises from the instinct of self-preservation implanted in us all – the same instinct which makes us jump out of the way of the oncoming bus. But when God gets tangled in the desire to succeed surely it's because we want not only to be conquerors, but righteous conquerors. We want to feel we deserve what we have won, that there should be no question of our having cheated or taken it from its proper owners merely by brute force.

So our victory-bringing god has to make ours the virtuous as well as the winning side – and it is here that one sees that a God of power, if power means to be able to over-power, is too narrow a concept for a life-ruler.

He makes no laws for satisfactory living except that one must never lose and never apologise. He takes no account of the suffering of the innocent, of those who do not see life as a battle and are prevented by pity from ever wishing to triumph, even if they happen for once to be in a position of strength. He gives courage, it's true, heroism, endurance and selflessness in battle, all the fighting virtues.

But he has no ideas for his followers once the cease fire has sounded. Consequently they often have to hand back control of all they have grasped to others who have little respect for conquerors' ideals.

In peacetime one notices the restlessness of industrial victors, of millionaires and entrepreneurs who chafe at having to pay taxes to keep those weaker and slower-witted than themselves; they are like frustrated buccaneers, living suspicious, guarded lives, afraid that others of their kind will try to take their wealth from them. And kidnappers, hijackers and blackmailers multiply, tempted by the smell of their success.

But must we promote a god of battle as the emblem of our philosophy? Must we see the world as a battlefield? I think not; many of us know that though the almighty is almighty, this is not the best aspect of his nature for man to worship. So tomorrow I turn to another aspect – that of the father.

The Loving Father

I began these reflections by quoting the Frenchman, Voltaire, who said that if there were no God, it would be necessary to invent him – and I've been imagining the kind of god we might invent. Yesterday I spoke of an almighty, a power-centred ruler, god of empires and conquerors.

Today I am thinking of another popular aspect of our home-made deity, the father-figure, the affectionate but just parent, who alternately praises and blames us, his children, but who almost never gives us up for lost.

There is a lot to be said for worshipping the fine qualities of parenthood. Maybe most devotion of all can be given to the total unselfishness of mothers who ask no return for their labour and loving care but merely that their children should flourish. But of course there is weakness in love so uncritical; to many a mother her child can do no wrong, and as we all know, this is a view rarely shared by the rest of society.

The father, on the other hand, is also traditionally the lawgiver, an impartial judge of conduct. To make him and his virtues one's god is to establish, one would think, a golden rule for daily life.

A father god means an ordered scheme of things, a family heirarchy in which he comes first, but in which everyone has his or her proper place. It also means a sensible discipline which will help the family stick together against its enemies or detractors. A father god will reward virtue and punish wrongdoers – but he is not everyone's notion of the ideal deity.

The weak spot in his overlordship is his likeness to human fathers. For one thing he may well have favourites, most fathers do; so he is not quite impartial. And he can also be a tyrant, ruling his household with a rod of iron, treating his wife and children like chattels, jealous of his sons, allowing no voice to be heard but his own. There are plenty of people who shudder at the memory of their father, and are far from enchanted at the thought of a divinity cast in such a mould.

Among Christians, the belief is that God is a loving father, a forgiver of unlimited mercy, but his paramount authority is not denied. Would this be the kind of God one should invent?

Perhaps the weakness in a total obedience to a father god is that it may give too little room for growing up spiritually.

I am thinking of the middle-aged daughter still clinging to her mother's apron-strings and waiting for parental approval before she does anything, or the son waiting increasingly hopelessly for his father to retire before he can run the family business or get married. These are cases where a really benevolent parent would have turned the child out to stand on his own feet and come to his own decisions.

An authoritative god, worshipped only in the personality of a father, can lead his adherents to mental laziness and a satisfied acceptance of things as they are, regardless of the most glaring need for change or adjustment. What is the use of murmuring 'Thy will be done' when what's needed to stop the car careering over a cliff is to put the brakes on?

Making a god for ourselves is not an easy piece of modelling; to shunt the responsibility for all we are and do on to our parents' shoulders, even if they are divine parents, may be interesting psychologically, but it is of little use to those who need a philosophy for a happy and fulfilled life.

So is there any other kind of deity we might invent who would answer all our needs? Tomorrow I will advance another candidate.

Mystic Chemistry

If there had been no god, we should have had to invent him – Voltaire's cynical remark on which I've been reflecting has kept many a doubter sitting uncomfortably on the religious fence, or sent many a devout believer down on his knees to ask himself whether the god he prays to is his own invention.

We do seize on particular aspects of divinity on which to

focus our faith; some who see life as a battle want a god who is a fighting ally, others who prefer not to waste time arguing about unknowable truths are prepared to accept the findings and the rule of a heavenly father, others who sense the presence of God all round them, but cannot see or grasp it – these, if they could, would make god a spirit.

It's easy enough to mock at such mystic chemistry. To say that god is love, or benevolence or the source of eternal life means nothing to many of us unless these qualities can be personified, made concrete and visible, to be depicted by artists, celebrated in music, visualised in human terms.

But consider a little further. Neither we nor our known universe is all beautiful, beneficent or creative by our standards. Malice, sickness, deformity, cruelty are as prevalent as righteousness. The deity to preside over us must be large enough to contain all opposites, good and bad, time and eternity, life and death.

God is a spirit to be worshipped in spirit and in truth, say the Christians, following their master, Jesus of Nazareth. But though we may, if we are Christians, try to save ourselves trouble by slavishly obeying Christ's precepts, we find that this is not enough. We are always thrown back on our own resources, made to ask questions about the way of the world and the laws of life which can only be answered through prayer and mental struggle.

If we would distil a spirit to be our god and king, we should have to look within ourselves and see how fearfully and wonderfully we have been made, for we are the only examples we know of our kind of being. What part of our spirit could safely be worshipped, what could take the blame for the ills of the universe, what would be worth preserving forever?

Our only guide can be what people have gained most from in this life – their children, probably, first, for the opportunity they provided for giving love, care and concern. And then, strangely enough, what we call evil – all the wrongs, ailments and opponents of our happiness which demand action in setting them to rights, finding cures for them, transforming them into friends. Where would the energetic amongst us be without crusades to organise and errors to correct? So selfless love and positive energy would mingle in a spiritual god. I would also keep the mystery, the puzzle about life's meaning which sends me back over and over again to question God, try to listen to Him and fathom the answers I begin to understand but can never grasp entirely.

No one has seen God, but all of us, I believe, know Him in some part of our being. When we try to formulate Him, it is out of our need to increase that knowledge and be filled more completely with the vital spirit of love.

Perhaps the most important point about us as god-makers is the one tremendous quality in our favour – the humility to recognise that we need help with our lives, that we cannot stand alone. It is a short step from the recognition of one's weakness to the discovery that there is help if we ask for it. Once one has had the barest inkling of God, it is impossible ever to forget or ignore it.

Better to wake up to the presence of the deity rather than try to fabricate it, no doubt. But either way, I would say, is preferable to indifference.